Unhiding My Skin

A Guidebook for LGBTQ+ Teens, Adults, and
Allies in The Radical Journey to
Self-Acceptance

Living Authentically

Loving Proudly

Inspiring Greatly

Carl Carado, Ed.D., RN

of the information contained within this document, including, but not limited to, errors, omissions, or inaccuracies.

To my parents, who persevered to pave a bright future for me. I hope you're proud of the person I have become as you watch me from above.

To my fellow courageous LGBTQ+ warriors, we come from different backgrounds, but we share so many similar stories that are powerful and inspirational.
I honor you.

To our LGBTQ+ allies.

To family members who have shown support and understanding through the years and to the friends who have become my chosen family.

To Matias, for loving me proudly and unconditionally.

"Don't let the expectations and opinions of other people affect your decisions. It's your life, not theirs. Do what matters most to you; do what makes you feel alive and happy. Don't let the expectations and ideas of others limit who you are. If you let others tell you who you are, you are living their reality — not yours. There is more to life than pleasing people. There is much more to life than following others' prescribed path. There is so much more to life than what you experience right now. You need to decide who you are for yourself. Become a whole being. Adventure."

— *Roy T. Bennett* (Author)

"I've been embraced by a new community. That's what happens when you're finally honest about who you are; you find others like you."

—*Chaz Bono* (Writer, Musician, Actor)

"When all Americans are treated as equal, no matter who they are or whom they love, we are all more free."-

—*Former United States President Barack Obama*

"**I** hate the word homophobia. It's not a phobia. You're not scared. You're an a**hole."

—*Morgan Freeman* (Actor)

"**N**ever be bullied into silence. Never allow yourself to be made a victim. Accept no one's definition of your life; define yourself."

—*Harvey Fierstein* (Actor, Playwright, Screenwriter)

"**A**ll of us who are openly gay are living and writing the history of our movement. We are no more - and no less - heroic than the suffragists and abolitionists of the 19th century; and the labor organizers, Freedom Riders, Stonewall demonstrators, and environmentalists of the 20th century. We are ordinary people, living our lives, and trying as civil-rights activist Dorothy Cotton said, to 'fix what ain't right' in our society."

—*United States Senator Tammy Baldwin (WI)*

"**M**y command is this:
Love each other as I have loved you. "

—*Jesus Christ* (John 15:12)

Table of Contents

Introduction

This is a guidebook written to encourage LGBTQ+ teenagers and adults to take action and move forward in their path to self-acceptance. In the title, I used the term 'radical,' which means 'pertaining to people who favor rapid and sweeping changes in laws and government.' (Merriam-Webster Dictionary) Why not apply this concept to our everyday lives? In my own experience as a gay man, I had to learn to love myself unconditionally. I continue to do my best in living a wholehearted life, which was my greatest source of inspiration when I was on my path to self-acceptance.

As an immigrant who came to this country full of hope like millions of others, this is my love letter to the LGBTQ+ community. There are a great many things included within the pages of this book and I sincerely hope that even while you read it, you will be able to reflect on your life. I want you to strengthen your growth as a person and how to accept yourself as the perfectly imperfect being that you are. Throughout this book, there will be discussion of difficult topics, including physical and sexual abuse, trauma, mental-health issues, and suicide.

Unfortunately, as LGBTQ+ individuals, these are things that we tend to be more susceptible to when compared with our straight and cisgendered allies. The bright side is that you can equip yourself with knowledge and awareness of these specific situations. On the other hand, it also highlights success stories, triumphs, and progress in advancing equality and acceptance. This guidebook also offers suggestions for resources that you can consider in order to address your needs, but it is neither the result of social science research nor a guidebook that addresses everything about the struggles of the LGBTQ+ community. Some of the information was cited from peer-reviewed research, articles, blogs, books, editorials, and website information from entities, including those focused on LGBTQ+ groups and allies. It would be an enormous honor for me if, after reading this book, you felt ready and eager to live your life fully and without regrets. You are a beautiful being. Now it is time to unhide your skin.

Chapter 1:

Unhiding Your Skin

Since it contrasted with the narrative of my life, I chose the title *Unhiding My Skin*. Through a series of life experiences that lasted for decades, it became my mission in life to unhide my skin, unbind myself from the constraints of fear and shame, and live my truth. I can recall hiding behind my skin as a young child (at five years old), as I first became aware of my differences. I instinctively understood the need for a defense mechanism to cover up what I perceived to be wrong.

The "incorrectness" of not feeling like doing what other little boys did at the time was a result of what I witnessed when I was a young child; when gay people in the country I grew up in were mistreated, taunted, harassed, negatively discussed, and made fun of. I was physically and verbally abused by neighborhood kids and at school even by teachers so frequently that I was unable to tell my parents about it because of shame and embarrassment. I felt that it was my fault.

Gay people were a constant presence in my family circle as some of them were our own relatives. A mother's instincts are generally correct, and this was evident when my mother told me later in life that from the moment I was conceived, she knew I would be different. For the most part, mothers are the first to notice these subtleties in their children. Growing up as a young teen in a predominantly Catholic country, even though my effeminate self was undeniable, the need for "hiding" was still necessary. I acted "straight" to save my life, so to speak, and to not offend my parents too much.

Although my mother was my defender, my father stayed quiet. They both had me later in their lives. My father was 50 when I was born. In fairness to my father, I have always felt his acceptance of me, or maybe he knew that he could not have done anything. As the youngest of nine children, and with four much older brothers, I can say that I sensed his protection. Whether that's accurate or not, I will live on with that belief. However, the world around me was cruel, and it was fair game outside my parents' protection.

My mother also initiated a change in our religious affiliation. We were introduced to the "born-again" sect and abandoned Catholic practices. At 15, I was baptized into the denomination and began participating in church activities. The fact remains that I was focused on developing my sense of self, and I made friends who were making the same discoveries as I was. Growing up, I was a singer who performed at church, school events, singing contests, the choir, and other venues. My ability to sing became a sort of social equalizer. For once, nobody thought I was disgusting or embarrassing

I attended an all-boys catholic high school, and I still recall singing the entire mass at graduation in front of around a thousand other students and guests. Even though it was evident that I was homosexual, one of my gay friends informed me that his parents still thought I sang well. If I hadn't been clearly gay, my friend claimed he wouldn't have denied I was his friend. The recollections were still so clear even though it had been more than 30 years earlier. Thinking about it now, there was never to be a social equalizer for this shame of not fitting the heteronormative society's model.

My elderly parents and I moved to the United States in the early 1990s. I was 19 years old at the time, and I was terrified. I was so naive and clueless. Once we arrived in Los Angeles, California, I found work, our family found a church, returned to school, finished my degree, and continued life. But I was still living a lie. I was still fighting the bible's promise of change. I relied on the bible verse in Romans Chapter 8 verse 28 that says, "All things work together for good to those who love God, to those who are called according to his purpose." But my genuine identity as a gay man has not been altered by years of service to the church and prayers.

I heard it in sermons that being gay is an abomination, it's a sin, and I'm going to hell. Those messages made me shudder, shrink, and I wanted the noise of condemnation within me to stop. I experienced a range of feelings, but at my worst moments, when I could not talk to anyone, I thought about killing myself to end my internal conflict. I questioned why I was even born. When I was in my 20s, I understood that I did not need to "pray the gay away." That's how I was created. However, I'll slink away when necessary and come out when I can be the person I was meant to be. My social circle was predominantly around other church friends. These people were not blind to the fact that I was gay, but somehow, I felt like they kept their judgments to themselves. I was fine for as long as I didn't flaunt it. I can keep on singing. I have no doubt that they probably prayed the gay away as well.

Later, following the events of 9/11, I was proud of our country and wanted to contribute in some way. So I joined the United States Army as a nurse officer and spent over a year in Germany during the height of the Middle East wars. Surprisingly, the military gave me the impression that it was acceptable to put on a show because military culture required a sense of order, demeanor, and behavior. Somehow, we were all actors as we complied with these directives daily. I wasn't bullied or harassed, most likely because I was an officer. Still, I had one of the best experiences of my life. I genuinely felt that for the first time, I felt like I belonged in a group where I could only assume that who you are, what you are, and where you come from didn't matter. I was proud to wear the uniform and as an immigrant, it was my absolute honor.

I felt that the friends I met in the military were genuine and didn't care that I was gay. The concept of "battle buddy" is precisely that. My survival was dependent on my buddy and vice versa. I can honestly say that I met many amazing people while serving in the military. At that point, I realized I could do anything and that my homosexuality shouldn't be an issue in the future. But that was, of course, wishful thinking. Outside the protections of the "Don't Ask, Don't Tell" policy of the military, life remained hostile to LGBTQ+ people.

Years later, my father died first, and my mother died a year and a half later. I left the military because, as much as I respected the institution, I was concerned that I would be constrained to live my full life. After all, the laws still prohibited openly gay people from serving at the time. And I can't go on like that. I did my duty and felt proud and privileged to have served. That was enough for me. Unfortunately, when I left, I also left behind the possibility of a distinguished military career and people who positively impacted my life.

I continued to live my authentic life cautiously. I dated, met other men, and felt I was in a good place. However, I've had disastrous relationships, but the experience led me to where I am today. I still knew that my family and church friends were against my so-called "lifestyle," but I just stopped caring anymore at that time. I finally fell in love and decided to get married to an amazing man. I emailed my family members to share my love story, future plans, and our wedding. Only two responded to send their best wishes. We planned our wedding, and it was the happiest day of our lives. We had nearly a hundred guests who shared and supported our journey. Sadly, I only invited one sister, and her family, who showed support for us and a few other relatives. The remainder were my husband's family, our closest friends, allies, and chosen family.

I shared a portion of my life story to demonstrate that we have control over our narrative. Sometimes we must take a leap of faith to get to the next rest stop. However, life is a process, and none of us can predict the future or be sure that our next decision will be the right one. At the end of the day, we have ourselves, our core beliefs, our authentic stories, and our desire to live a fulfilled life. But we need to hear more of our stories. There is always a lesson to be learned, a nugget to inspire, or an experience that can change a life for good. I know that my life experiences—all of them—have changed me for the better.

As you read this book, I encourage you to have an open mind and remember that the purpose of this book is to offer real-life perspectives and information for LGBTQ+ teens and adults in their journey to self-acceptance. It is based on my personal story as well as my takeaways and inspiration from others, and available sources. There may be triggering words that bring back unpleasant memories and stories that may offer ideas you have not considered before.

I continue by honoring the words of the late Maya Angelou: "Let choice whisper in your ear and love murmur in your heart. Be ready. Here comes life." My hope is that you come out of this experience with a renewed sense of hope that there is life beyond self-acceptance that we all should look forward to. Your situation today may be difficult but like many of us in the LGBTQ+ community, we continue to survive and thrive at the same time.

Life Awaits: It's Your Time

Every person in this world was born with certain qualities: gender identity and sexual orientation are included in this. Some people can argue that it is inappropriate to have traits that are different from the norm. However, this way of thinking must be challenged one person at a time. Our lived experience of who we are should not be diminished just because it does not make sense to others, or they simply refuse to understand. I personally believe that none of us would voluntarily impose pain and suffering inflicted by society in general just by being LGBTQ+ if our sexual orientation or sexual identity was a choice. Better yet, why do specific characteristics occur naturally if they are unwanted or unnatural?

Unhiding our skin represents telling our unique story. Stories that have influenced us since we first realized there was a conflict between how we understood ourselves and how we saw the people around us. Furthermore, it also focuses on how we place ourselves in our own homes, schools, groups, friendships, workplaces, and other environments where interacting with others is necessary. Our entry into the world, where we first share traits with our family, begins with our birth. Our family unquestionably gave us our identity and the confidence that we are a part of a group. The bulk of us have experienced the innocence of belonging to a single unit in varied degrees, filled with love, security, and a sense of protection.

Despite being a part of a family with many similarities, we became more aware of how different we were as we matured. We learned that we have inherent qualities that we may only be aware of ourselves and that have not yet been identified by others. We began to understand that people perceive and react to our thoughts and feelings in varied ways depending on how we think, perceive, and communicate them. All of this appears to be stunning and fantastic. We all try to live authentic lives, but we have one thing in common: other people frequently don't like it when we do. So, we felt the need to protect our true identities and skins from harm, as they didn't conform to societal molds, which meant sacrificing a life of freedom.

Accepting who we naturally are—who we are inside, despite social constraints—is the straightforward first step in the journey to stop hiding behind our skins. Remember that millions of other people worldwide are like you, no matter where your path leads or who you ultimately discover yourself. Like you, these people are either learning to love themselves or already do. Some of them haven't even started their process yet: remember, learning requires knowledge. Knowledge and education are what keep humanity alive. Therefore, to understand and learn about oneself is to be human.

It's Not Your Choice: You Were Born This Way

I was in awe of all the different facets of a person's personality as a child. I knew that we were all different in many ways, even though I had no knowledge of psychology or human behavior. Yet, I was able to make a friend with whom I could go on enjoyable adventures and play games all day. Basic human requirements were extremely socially unequal where I grew up. The social equalizer, nevertheless, was the love of one's neighborhood.

As children, all we wanted to do was play and explore the area all day. We didn't give a damn about our parents' backgrounds or whether I had a secure home life compared to my buddies. But ever since I can remember, I also knew that gay people existed because my friends, family, and other community members have pointed out the differences. I didn't know at that time what that meant, but I only knew that it meant that gay people were both taunted and tormented while also being welcomed as community members. I equate that today to the word "tolerance" although not entirely accurate. It was also then that I realized I may be just like them.

Though there are continuing debates and studies about the nature of sexual orientation and gender identity, you must be convinced of one truth–you were born this way. Being gay or transgender is not a choice offered to you. It is something that happens to people naturally. Though many studies claim that homosexuality or transgender issues, for example, are not 'natural,' you need to focus and remember–how you feel, perceive, and see yourself. Your body comes from the innermost being that only you can manifest externally.

For example, let's say you are a teenage boy. You have only just gone through puberty. Your friends around you are starting to be attracted to girls your age. On the other hand, you have just noticed Justin–a cute transfer student. He plays on the football team, so you want to go to all of his games. You have a crush on him and are physically attracted to him–not because you decided you would be, but because your pulse races when he speaks to you. Your pupils dilate whenever he smiles. Physically, your body is reacting to him.

This is natural and normal, no matter what the studies say otherwise. Forcing yourself to pretend to like girls, in this case, would do you a disservice; you would not be listening to your body, heart, or soul. You would be lying to yourself and others.

Attraction is just like any emotion—it affects us physically and mentally. For example, if you are angry, you might grow hot in the cheeks, your brows furrow, and you might ball your hands up into fists. These are all physical reactions your body automatically goes through. Just like when you are happy—your eyes light up, you laugh, you grin or smile. When you are sad, you cry. When you are gay, you are attracted to the same sex.

The main thing to remember is that you cannot deceive yourself. You cannot misrepresent who you really are to yourself. Even though some people will believe you are lying or that something is wrong with you, keep in mind that you must live your truth. You must accept and love who you are, including your reactions. Researchers found that older bisexuals and lesbians, especially those who had grown up in a culture that did not view homosexuality as natural, thought lesser of themselves and their sexualities. In contrast, younger women who had grown up understanding that their sexualities are natural had more self-esteem (Morandini et al., 2017).

There is also the issue of violence committed against LGBTQ+, which contributes to demoralization that can be made worse in the absence of social support. Sexual assault is more common among people who identify as gay or as part of the LGBTQ+ community. Unfortunately, persons who identify as transgender or bisexual women tend to face this more frequently. This shows that accepting yourself and your sexuality or gender identity–or both–as natural is extremely important to happiness and personal growth.

As you read this book, you'll learn that it supports the fact that you were born exactly the way you are. Whatever your sexual orientation or gender identity—whether you've accepted it or are still unsure—the reality is that you've already acknowledged your individuality. This is the stage of the self-discovery and understanding process that some people find the most difficult. The last step is discovering how to live your best life, authentically, without uncertainty, and discomfort.

Once again, you were, without a doubt, born this way.

There Is Nothing to Fix About You

You are, undoubtedly, the person you were born to be. The word "fix" denotes something to be repaired. I must admit that this is a loaded word that can be taken from so many different directions. Nevertheless, it signals that there's something wrong with me and that I cannot function properly unless I am repaired. We don't need to be "fixed" just by being LGBTQ+. While I have no doubt that most of us know that we have other aspects in our lives that may require some repair, being LGBTQ+ is not one of them.

The American Psychiatric Association (APA) did away with the diagnosis of "homosexuality" in its Diagnostic and Statistical Manual's (DSM) second edition in 1973 (Drescher, 2015). This resulted from conflicting attitudes toward homosexuality between those that pathologize it and those that view it as natural. The stigma of years ago that classifies homosexuality as a psychiatric condition is still traumatic, especially for those who lived it. Therefore, your sexual orientation or gender identity needs no repair regardless of what you've heard or read.

We are expected to fit into a lot of molds in society. The environment we live in anticipates that we will maintain the status quo and keep our heads down, but that is not how things work in nature. Sometimes, you're not the person that other people want you to be.

Because of this, we frequently experience mockery, rejection, persecution, embarrassment, or isolation. All of these things happen to us because we do not conform to social norms.

You remain a human being, nevertheless. Love and acceptance are things you yearn for and need. Any other person has the same desires as you have. There's nothing to correct, and you don't have to fit any molds or roles. It is sufficient to just be. Despite what society may try to convince you of, you are sufficient on your own.

The great thing about being human is that we all have the exact basic needs and desires—yet, we are all vastly different. There is no one right way to be a human.

You were born into this world with flaws, regardless of what god you believe in—or don't believe in—and what texts or rituals govern your existence. You were created to live in harmony with other flawed people. As valid as they are, so are you. There is nothing wrong with you because we are all just people.

Others may tell you a lot that needs fixing, but that is their viewpoint. They genuinely believe that. You are not required to adopt their views. You are equally as excellent and flawed as they are. We all strive to survive, find love in some form and live happy, secure lives where we feel like we belong. Yes. Just like everyone else, you have a place here on this planet.

As a person, you are entirely fallible. Because of this, there is nothing that must be fixed about you. By embracing this, you dispel anyone else's notion that you are fundamentally "wrong." This lack of confidence has plagued me in all that I've done for a very long time. Unfortunately, it does it occasionally, even today. However, my core conviction that I don't need to be fixed evens the playing field, so I think it never goes away.

Being gay is not a choice, which many people don't seem to comprehend. Because of biological elements beyond our control and ingrained in us from birth, our sexual orientations are part of nature's genetic masterplan and unique to each human being (Cook, 2020). This is revealed in the following by the article by Planned Parenthood (2022):

> A person cannot change their sexual orientation through counseling, therapy, or persuasion since it is not something they choose. Also impossible is for someone to "become gay." For instance, a

boy won't become gay if he plays with dolls or other toys that are generally intended for girls.

Many people's sexuality is also a moving target, so you can now find yourself drawn to guys. However, as time passes, you discover that you are also drawn to women (Katz-Wise, 2022). It's possible that you initially find that you are attracted to women but subsequently discover that you are not. All humans experience this fluidity, though not all people go through it. It is normal and natural. Because their sexual orientations have changed throughout their lives, even persons who identify as straight have had relationships with people of the same sex.

Every single thing about this is normal and natural. The fluidity and change that characterizes human beings. Everything in this situation only has to be accepted and embraced; nothing needs to be fixed.

Journey to Honesty

The discussion about the road to honesty is critical. I must emphasize that this is here without any negative connotation or judgment, especially since some of you may not have come out yet. I have to say that I am inspired by your strength of character for making such challenging decisions on your own. Fear of the unknown is terrible. We all deserve to take a step toward honesty as part of self-acceptance. To reveal my true skin required stormy back-and-forth mental gymnastics with myself and an almost perpetual balancing act to accomplish self-preservation. I lied about who I was in the process, yet I got nothing in return besides hurt and disappointment. Lying or keeping my sexual orientation a secret never served me. But because of my anxiety over being rejected and humiliated, I felt compelled to do it repeatedly. It was difficult to stop those lying times because terror always won.

Being completely honest with ourselves and others may occasionally not be possible in our relationships. We want to present "us" and "you" in the best possible light. So, we're doing this. You might occasionally fall short in one or more of these areas. We may lie to our loved ones and ourselves due to this way of thinking. Behind a mask, we begin to skulk. I can recall making a concerted effort to behave like other "normal" boys to avoid standing out and becoming the target of bullying. While my buddies embraced me, the world outside that small group was a battleground. Each day was a delicate balance. The pressure was way too much to handle.

Yet we must take off that mask to experience true happiness in life. With those we love, we must be upfront and honest about who we are—and perhaps more importantly, who we are within. Humans are all distinctly different, even though society pushes us to fit into molds and to be like sheep.

Honesty can only be attained one step at a time. You must first take the necessary action to acknowledge that there is only one specific version of you and that we are all singular creatures composed of complex physical and emotional systems. The steps you take to become your true self should be thrilling and fulfilling in and of themselves, yet this path does take time and dedication.

Let's take a brief detour through history. Human society has been on the road to self-awareness and honesty for a very long time. For instance, a group of Christian monks known as the Desert Fathers strived to be aware of themselves and their openness during the fourth century in Egypt. One of the things they did to put this into reality was to give their inner shadows names; in other words, they tried to provide a name to the energy they kept inside.

These monks' feelings and thoughts were not regarded as sins when these shadows were identified and presented to the leader of the Desert Fathers, Abba. Thus, for instance, if one perceived their shadow as lust, they would sit down and attempt to ascertain why that person felt lustful rather than banishing that person as a sinner.

They perceived these things as being a part of the human condition. They took these shadows and dissected them for better understanding and ensuring that their feelings were genuine with both themselves and others. They were never regarded as being immoral or evil. Instead, they were something that had to be exposed for analysis and understanding.

The Desert Fathers left us with the notion that we are not exempt from having shadows. There are things about us that we have been told are wrong, things we should bury, dismiss, or atone for. But we are made up of various components, much like our skin. Locking away that feeling, or thought would mean locking away a piece of you. Bring it out into the open, understand why it makes you feel that way, and embrace that it is a part of you.

What role does this play in your quest for honesty? How does this relate to the debate over LGBTQ+ people? Homosexuality has long been seen by society as one of those evil forces. Many of us have seen a hint of the shadow due to the stain surrounding who we are. After stuffing it away, we locked the door. We lied to everyone around us and to ourselves.

You would realize now that it is just a part of yourself, not a demon or a shadow if you were to bring that aspect into the light. It is a loving aspect of you that deserves to be honored. So, therefore, you too, must come out of the shadows if you're going to be sincere and genuine with yourself.

There is nothing about you that resembles a shadow. You are more than that; you are worth more than simply a shelf in a cluttered closet.

You get clarity, strength, and the audacity to move forward with your life in a way that suits you when you are honest with yourself. Being truthful with yourself requires you to open and acknowledge the aspects of yourself that society would have you overlook. Accept yourself as you are. Don't be harsh with yourself for things you can't change.

Self-awareness allows you to recognize your identity and your distinctiveness. So, stop keeping yourself hidden away.

Even if you put on a front to be someone you know you are not, when you are honest with yourself, you will be happy with who you are. You won't worry about what others think of you as you express your true self (Pearce, 2019). This is because, in the end, you can conceal your truth from the outside world but not yourself. Therefore, to be proud of who you are, you must stay loyal to yourself. Being truthful with yourself allows you to accept your shortcomings, most of which you're already familiar with.

You may be aware of both your strengths and weaknesses. People's opinions of you can become less significant if you have enough self-awareness. Because the world and other people's opinions can't bring you down when you know your skills, you can grow braver. For example, suppose someone tells you that you can't achieve something, but you know you can. In that case, your confidence will probably not be affected, allowing you to move forward fearlessly to achieve your objectives.

Our Stories Together

Since the beginning of human communication, stories have been crucial because stories let us relate and make sense of our experiences. We have shared stories with one another throughout time and space. Face-to-face, around campfires, through songs, drawings on cave walls, and to relatives and strangers are all ways we communicate with them. We are influenced and engaged by stories. However, we rarely consider the significance, authenticity, and depth that the storyteller adds to the story or the power of storytelling (ASAP, 2019).

When we have an experience, our brains search for a narrative to explain it. We gain knowledge from the experiences of others and from stories that explain. In the brain, imagined events are treated the same way as actual ones. According to neuroscientific studies, our brains release the stress hormone cortisol when a story is tense. When we watch cute animal videos, oxytocin—the chemical that fosters connection and empathy—is released. When a story has a happy ending, dopamine is released, which promotes optimism and hope (ASAP, 2019).

This means that you are not alone and that there is a narrative out there that will capture your attention, motivate you, and ignite a fire inside you despite how difficult it may be. Millions of people worldwide are currently going through the same thing as you are. Even though our life experiences may be diverse, I believe that being gay is a part of what makes us all human. Similarly, members of the LGBTQ+ community are just as many people as anyone else.

Therefore our personal stories are so important. When you tell your story to the world, someone, somewhere, is listening. Your story might reach someone on the other side of the world. Sharing your experience might change someone's life—and your story becomes a part of theirs.

Let's imagine that you come out on social media. You finally come out as bisexual, for example. You're dating a person of the same gender as you. Your tale has been told. You get a notification from one of your followers the next day. He gained the confidence to reveal to his family that he is gay thanks to your story.

Your story, in this case, changed the world for someone else. By showing the world your true self, by refusing to hide, you gave someone else the courage to do the same. You let your follower know that he isn't alone. That is powerful. And it is easily spread to make a difference to save another life if we hear more about it from others. That is awe-inspiring.

In telling your story, you might have also opened the eyes of those around you. Those who know you now understand you a bit better. They can see where you are coming from—and for some, you might have opened their eyes. You have allowed them to begin to understand. Listening to stories is just as important as telling them. By listening to someone else, you will gain a point of view that you didn't have before. This allows you to find common ground with the person telling the story in the same way that they understand you better when you tell yours.

Stories also promote healing. There are many ways that this is true. For example, if you and someone you know do not see eye to eye all the time, sharing your own personal stories can lead you to understand each other better. Maybe you tell your story to someone in your family who does not agree with your sexual orientation or does not understand what it means. When you tell your story, you express your lived experience in the most authentic and emotion-filled way. However, telling your story can be a scary thing.

It took me so many years in my adulthood to realize there is nothing shameful about my story. I shouldn't feel bad about standing up for myself. I may disappoint people whose main priority was to have me become more like their idea of being "normal" or "straight" so that life is more manageable.

Dr. Brene Brown, a social science researcher who studied shame, once said that shame is like a gremlin that says we are not good enough. She added that we can quiet that gremlin down when we go in, walk the path, and say to ourselves, "I'm going to do this."

An online post poignantly stressed that the most effective teaching method for persuading and understanding one another is through storytelling. When knowledge or experience is tied to a narrative, we can better recall it and draw connections.

Most partnerships begin with us telling stories about ourselves to introduce ourselves and build a bond (Boris, 2017). Others will also share their stories and open to you when you do so that we can all relate to and comprehend one another.

Our stories represent the courage to go uphill to live authentically. Therefore, when you tell your story, those willing to listen will realize that, just like theirs, our sexual identity isn't a choice. It is not something to be guilty of because it's a stamp we have always carried from the time we were conceived in our mother's womb.

Here are some examples of powerful LGBTQ+ stories (Olito, 2020).

- Jordan Steffy, a gay teen, was caught on video standing up to his bully, and the internet called him a hero.

- Dynasia Clark protested her high school graduation after she was told she had to wear a dress.

- A Christian summer camp fired Jace Taylor because of his sexuality, and he issued an inspiring call to action.

- Seth Owen, a high school valedictorian, was concerned that he wouldn't be allowed to attend college after being expelled from his house due to his to his sexual orientation until his instructors intervened.

- At the age of 19, LGBT adolescent Keegan Roberts is one of the youngest elected officials in the US.

- Benton Sorensen revealed his gender identity during a class presentation.

- Tom Sosnik, 13, also came out during an emotional speech at school.

- Gia Fisher wrote an emotional letter to her school about coming out, and the response was encouraging.

- Evan Young intended to come out during his graduation speech as valedictorian. While his school forbade it, he yet persisted.

- After asking out the straight football captain of his high school, Alexander Duarte's "promposal" went viral.

- The election of Craig Cassey as prom king, he claimed, was a sign of acceptance for the LGBTQ+ community.

Despite all the odds, these young people have managed to conquer their worries and demonstrate to the world how fortunate we are to hear their stories. These aren't just sweet tales; they're stories of hope, survival, and triumph in the face of dangers to one's physical, mental, and emotional security. These are only a handful of the countless stories that exist and cover a vast range of human experiences and feelings.

The Path We Choose Is the Beginning of Unhiding

Not everyone's journey is going to look the same. There is no one right way to unhide your own skin. You might be ready when someone else is not; someone else will be telling their story when you are still hiding away.

That is okay.

The critical thing to remember is that everyone's story is a little different. However, you will know when the right time to unfurl yourself is because your emotions, thoughts, and convictions will empower you.

In peeling back the layers that you have used to cover your actual skin, you will find that you will also release many things that have held you back. It is a freeing experience that you should be proud of having gone through.

I remember how I felt when I finally believed that the path I chose in life was to find someone to love and be loved in return. I felt the release of so many uncertainties, the back-and-forth balancing of beliefs and principles I was forced to learn and believe in. But, in the end, the real me prevailed, and I chose the path of freedom from the "gremlins" in my shadows that have held me back.

Each of the layers you remove represents a variety of things, such as years of inner turmoil, anguish, fear, guilt, rage, and other feelings and ideas buried deep within you. You will come into yourself by shedding these layers as a reptile sheds its old skin. Underneath the dead cells, you will find that your natural skin glistens and shines in the light. And there you are. The beautiful you!

An online blog post suggested that we cannot continuously play a part. It's a mask that conceals this. I found myself at a crossroads where I had to decide between continuing to lie and living in dread and separation or coming clean and taking the chance of being rejected (Stewart, 2019).

Do you wish to play a role for the rest of your life? Or do you want to move on, stop playing pretend, and face yourself as who you really are? We are not actors on stage, but these stage plays are based on our powerful stories. We are the truth behind the fiction.

There are many things that we might do in life that we use a mask for. Maybe at work, you must be stern and professional, even though you are a very loving and funny person. There might be social situations in which you have to be gentle and caring, even though you really would like to tell your friend to dump her girlfriend. We wear masks during moments like these—but in being ourselves, our true selves, we should not have to.

Anything that you do that is related to accepting yourself will always be the right decision. Let's go with the first example from above of being a manager at work. You must be stern with your workers, telling them what tasks they must complete every day. This wears on you, as underneath that manager's mask, you are a loving, caring, and funny person.

As a manager, you do not have to come off as a robot. You can still do your job, and do it well, while maintaining your personal outlook on life. You might spend some time getting to know your workers, listening to them when they have issues outside of work that will, eventually, affect their work. You can crack a few jokes here and there, and all in all be a nice person while still being stern enough to make sure that the work gets done.

In this way, you can perform your job well without the need for a mask. This goes for anything in life, really, including being LGBTQ+. You can be yourself while at work, or around friends and family. By embracing who you really are, you can take off that mask all together, leaving you free to feel at ease in your correct skin. There will be times when, for safety, you might have to cover yourself again—but know that those times will be fleeting.

When you accept yourself fully and unconditionally, you will feel better. You will fit into yourself in a way that you never were able to before. It is like slipping into a pair of pants you wore in high school that you never thought you would be able to wear again. It takes time and effort, but in the end, you will look amazing in those pants—just as you feel amazing in your own, unhidden skin.

This is not just about coming to terms with your sexuality or your gender identity. Anything that is related to accepting yourself will help you continue in the correct direction. For example, there are many people out there who would love to wear a certain style of clothing, but for some reason or another, they don't. Instead, they wear clothing that makes them feel horrible about themselves.

The best thing to do in that situation is throw caution to the wind. Dress the way you want to. Maybe you usually dress in sweatpants and a sweatshirt, but you really would love to rock some stiletto heels and skinny jeans. There should be nothing holding you back–dress how you like to, when you can. If other people have an issue with it, then that is their problem. You should feel as comfortable in your clothing as you should in your own skin. This, too, is a moment of acceptance.

Unhiding that natural skin of yours is only the beginning. You will soon learn how to find yourself and accept yourself just as you are. Once you have learned how to love and accept yourself, you can start to heal.

It's time to take off the mask and free yourself from hiding!

Chapter 2:

Claiming Your Rightful

Place

Every single one of us belongs. No one on this Earth is alone on an island. But, though some of us may feel like outcasts, we still often find solace in one another. As human beings, we are tied to a shared identity called humanity. But sadly, being surrounded by other humans sometimes does not mean achieving a sense of belonging (Brower, 2021).

The subject of faith has received negative attention in the LGBTQ+ community, especially for those of us who hold religious beliefs. After all, religion is often tied to guilt, fear, anger, or shame; some opinions claim that homosexuality is a sin and should be condemned. This hatred has influenced so many people across all nations today. The continuous attack and harmful threats in varying forms continue to destroy and take lives away. I can certainly understand how this can hold you back. It froze me so often that I felt a pit in my stomach.

On the other hand, certain cultures are tied to a strong belief in the supernatural that shows an understanding of the role of gay people in their communities. For example, in Samoan culture, the term "third gender," which means "in the manner of a woman," is fa'afafine. The Samoa

Fa'afafine Association claims that it is ingrained in Polynesian culture and has been a feature of island life for as long as anybody can remember. Most communities in Samoa's villages have fa'afafine, which number in the thousands. Boys who are visibly effeminate are likely to be taught the traditional responsibilities of Samoan women, which frequently involve housework.

Although sex between men is illegal in Samoa, and wearing women's clothing is socially unacceptable, the fa'afafine community is allowed to cross these barriers. Even though most contemporary fa'afafine partner with males, the identity makes no claims on sexual orientation. The bond between the fa'afafine and the church is fragile and occasionally tense. The church embraced the fa'afafine, and many contributed to the congregations. However, fa'afafine was regarded by the church as male, and same-sex unions were not encouraged by the church (Barrett, 2019).

How, then, can one believe in a god or subscribe to a religious faith while also being faithful to themselves?

Your Own Faith Journey

Although I was baptized in the Catholic church as an infant, I was also ceremoniously baptized as part of a fundamentalist Christian church as a teen. As I mentioned at the beginning of the book, my mother's influence and how her life has changed because of this renewed commitment to God became the pivotal point for my three sisters and me to share in that experience. The phrase "born-again" has encompassed my life as a young teen. I grew up in a family of Catholics, and my mother spearheaded us to enter a sect called "born-again" Christians.

For the sake of being true to the mission of this book, I will not delve into a deep discussion of Christianity but express my view on how it has impacted me. I don't profess to be a biblical scholar; however, what I learned attending vacation bible schools and bible studies reminded me of this biblical passage.

According to John 3:5-7: "Jesus answered, I tell you the truth, no one can enter the kingdom of God unless he is born of water and Spirit. Flesh gives birth to flesh, but the Spirit gives birth to Spirit. You should not be surprised at my saying; you must be born again." As explained, it means the awakening in all of us as believers to the actual presence of the Holy Spirit in our daily lives (Washington, 2021). Sadly, the symbolic meaning of this "rebirth" in Christ has been associated with a lot of things in politics, discrimination, and hatred, especially in these heightened societal times, except for its authentic biblical meaning.

Biblical passages such as this have been used as a sword by some extreme religious leaders to target people like us, who in their opinion, live contrary to its biblical teachings. Many biblical scholars have had the guts to assert that the Bible does not condemn homosexuality and that the New Testament does not adopt a clearly stated position on homosexuality (Scroggs, 1983). I acknowledge my prejudice in writing this merely due to the suffering I have gone through for so many years because of using scripture as a one-sided shield with a constrained understanding of the context.

For those of us raised in the Christian faith, according to Philippians 2:4, we should consider both our own interests and other people's interests. Additionally, Jesus says in Matthew 5 that if someone makes you go one mile, go two miles with them. If only we could persuade those who rejected us but shared our beliefs, to travel a short distance with us even though it would be uncomfortable. We identify as LGBTQ+. It wasn't a decision we made. This was never about a choice, not because it's necessarily a horrible thing to choose. But being different and feeling misunderstood and unaccepted can be incredibly unpleasant, stressful, challenging, and frequently lonely. Some of us, or perhaps most of us, may have grown up in a secure and loving family and home. Some people may still adore their parents, and the fortunate ones may still have close bonds with both. Some of us might not have ever been married. But some of us also have the greatest desire to be married, have a lifelong partner, and have a family.

Personally, suppose I were to use the traditional interpretation of Scripture. In that case, the potential of love, companionship, and the possibility of raising a family is denied to me. The conventional interpretation of Scripture also holds that falling in love is among the worst things that may happen to a gay person. You will need to flee because you will inevitably be devastated, and this will occur each time you develop excessive affection for someone else. You will constantly be excluded from romantic relationships, marriages, and family beginnings. The delights of having a spouse and kids of your own are things that you will never experience personally. This means that we will always be alone. I have come to accept that I was not created to be alone. I can love someone of the same sex and want a loving, honest, and intimate relationship with another man. That is part of my purpose and an intentional design by God that is free from defects.

As a young teen, I was told I had the gift of singing. I served in praise-and-worship teams for decades since then, while grappling with my distorted view of my sexual orientation and what the bible was telling me. I have no doubt that hundreds, if not thousands, of people I met through the years have prayed to God to take the "gay away" from me. However, God has a better plan of giving me the strength and perseverance to be true to who I am first because I was created in His image and likeness. This is between Him and me. I struggled with self-acceptance as an LGBTQ+ child, and I have experienced being shamed in church. I continue to experience rejection and hatred as an LGBTQ+ adult. It led me to stay away from religious institutions and gatherings, but my faith never left me. I had to believe and receive Jesus' assurance of love, acceptance, and belonging for all of us. Plain and simple, with no strings attached.

When thinking about your faith, the most important thing to remember is that your relationship with your higher power is your own. Your relationship with religion is entirely up to you—no one can tell you how or not to worship. This might be difficult to understand at first—religions have rules.

Wherever the sources of inspiration may have come from to form religions, humans created them. Their culture influenced their teachings, which did not anticipate advancing science, knowledge, and understanding of human development and behaviors thousands of years later. Remember that.

The Council of Europe described religion and belief as composed of many faith myths, symbols, rituals, and histories. They were meant to explain the beginning of the universe or life or provide meaning for life. Their beliefs about the cosmos and human nature often serve as the foundation for their morality, ethics, religious regulations, or preferred way of life. Numerous religions have clergy, congregations of the laity, regular worship services or gatherings for the veneration of a deity or prayer, holy sites (either natural or artificial), and scriptures. They also have organized behaviors, sacred places (either natural or artificial), and a definition of what constitutes adherence or membership.

What people believe is up to them, and how you communicate or honor your greater power is up to you. That relationship, that thread that connects you to something greater—no one can take that from you. That is between you and your higher power. In the Bible, Jesus also said, "I give you a new commandment: love one another. Just as I have loved you, you must also love one another" (John 13:34). The apostle Paul then wrote, "Love does no wrong to a neighbor. Love, therefore, is the fulfillment of the law" (Rom. 13:10). In my opinion, this text says it all and requires no further interpretation.

Love supersedes everything. It should not be conditional; your higher power understands that and never only love you because of one specific thing, nor will they ever cast you aside for something else. The love is unconditional and faithful. You deserve that love.

Simply said, you deserve to be cherished. Respect and acceptance are due to you. You are entitled to your place in society. You must grant yourself permission to feel safe and secure since you have a right to do so. Do not let anything that you may deem to be imperfect keep you back.

Every human on Earth is equally alive and deserving of love and acceptance. You are not alone—remember that. Though our experiences might be similar, we all have different stories. Yet, underneath all of that, we are all human beings. We all deserve to be loved, to be heard, and to be seen.

It should be noted as well that many organized religions are slowly starting to understand and accept people who are in the LGBTQ+ community. Still, as human beings, whereas before, they were not accepted by many religious organizations in the United States (Human Rights Campaign, 2011).

It's fantastic that religious institutions are beginning to acknowledge and accept us. It is particularly crucial because research has shown that LGBTQ+ kids frequently experience high-stress levels related to being accepted by their religious communities (Page et al.,

2013). When our religious communities stop seeing homosexuality as a crime, it allows us to flourish. We do not have to hide out of fear or shame; instead, we can worship with our friends, family, and other loved ones as we were intended to do in the first place.

However, a rising number of established religious organizations in the United States have recently released declarations formally embracing LGBTQ+ individuals as members. Additionally, a lot of religious institutions have supported causes that concern LGBTQ+ people in America, including the struggle against discrimination, the legalization of same-sex unions, and the ordination of openly LGBTQ+ clergy.

Similarly, those of us who are transgender, or gender non-conforming have started to find safe spaces within our religious communities (Sandstrom, 2015). There is still a lot of misunderstanding and hate. Still, LGBTQ+ people are slowly starting to be accepted in areas and communities where we were previously shunned. There is hope.

Religion has provided comfort and misery for many lesbians, gay, bisexual, transgender, and queer Americans. Many LGBTQ+ Americans raised in organized faith still respect their faith community. However, many have been forced to leave because lesbian, gay, and bisexual people are rejected by these groups.

The Impact of Anger, Fear, Guilt, Shame, Doubt

It is normal and natural to feel myriad emotions as you begin your journey. However, you will find your rightful place within your social circle, religious community, and society.

These emotions might include anger. This anger is likely directed at yourself for knowing who you are and not allowing yourself to show yourself. That anger might also be directed at society for not allowing you to be yourself. You felt rejection and shame—someone may have harmed you physically when you attempted to show your true self.

It is essential to acknowledge the trauma caused by these experiences and emotions. However, you should not have to go through that trauma alone–there are many different resources that you can contact to help you. These include professional counselors, therapists, and groups that specialize in aiding LGBTQ+ people living with emotional and physical trauma. For example, the Trevor Project is a non-profit organization that provides information and support to young people 24 hours a day and 365 days a year.

It is also essential to stay safe. As you develop and show your courage daily, you must also know that violence against LGBTQ+ people has increased over the past few years.

Rejection of any kind is painful. It can be even more painful when that rejection comes from those you love, like family members or close friends. However, there is hope in overcoming this pain and sacrifice; you are internally stronger than you think. Your inner strength and your found community are critical tools for coming into yourself and unhiding your skin.

This is not to say that being rejected by your family will cause no pain to you as an individual. A study on LGBTQ+ youth between the ages 14 to 24 has shown that parental rejection can cause issues in identification (Bregman et al., 2012). Simply put, this means that those of us sadly rejected by our parents tend to have problems with self-identifying who we are. It hurts to admit that we are homosexuals.

Yet there is hope. Research has also shown that LGBTQ+ youth tend to stick together and forge resilient and meaningful bonds. These younger individuals have been found to take the pain of rejection and turn it into a positive outcome. They have found a way to turn the negativity they have received into resilience (Asakura, 2016). In such darkness and hopelessness, they found light and hopefulness.

Sadly, sexual orientation or gender-identity trauma has affected many of us in the LGBTQ+ community. This is also likely to be the case for trauma that we may face in the future. This trauma includes, but is not limited to bullying, harassment, physical and sexual abuse, social rejection, and intolerance. And over 29% of LGBTQ+

teenagers have either left their homes, had their homes forcibly taken away from them, or have been homeless, claims a report (Psychcentral, 2021). In addition, people who identify as gay or as part of the LGBTQ+ community experience sexual assault more frequently than the general population. It is also alarming that transgender and bisexual women experience sexual assault more frequently.

People in the LGBTQ+ community must deal with violence against them more often than individuals outside the community. Worse yet, the violence against the community has increased over the last few years, including the 2016 shooting at the Pulse Nightclub in Florida (American Psychiatric Association, n.d.). In the aftermath of the shooting, 49 people were killed, with another 53 injured because of one man's hatred for LGBTQ+ persons.

One year later, according to an article from the American Psychiatric Association, violent attacks against the LGBTQ+ community had increased by a terrifying 86% from 2016 (American Psychiatric Association, n.d.). Transgender people–especially those of color–tend to be hit harder by hate crimes than other community members. In 2019 alone, a reported 15 black trans women were killed (American Psychiatric Association, n.d.).

In 2017, 129 anti-LGBTQ+ bills were introduced across 30 states—these bills ranged from adoption laws to laws regarding 'religious freedoms' and heavily impacted the

LGBTQ+ community (American Psychiatric Association, n.d.).

Going further, those of us in the LGBTQ+ community face harassment early on. Many of us within the community have reported being harassed while in school, ranging from kindergarten to our senior year of high school. Some of this harassment includes physical assault, and some also include sexual assault. As children, we are supposed to feel safe and secure within the walls of our schools. Instead, for many of us, those walls become like prison bars. We are trapped with our aggressors, unable to leave and forced to take the punishment we receive for trying to be ourselves. Most recently, the November 2022 mass shooting by a 22-year-old gunman at Club Q, an LGBTQ+ club considered a safe space in Colorado Springs, took the lives of 5 people, and injured more than a dozen. Included among those killed were LGBTQ+ persons and allies. The terroristic act had all the trappings of a hate crime according to police reports.

This harassment and discrimination can often continue to follow us into the workforce. We are often faced with being overlooked for promotions. In 27 states, there are no explicit statewide laws protecting LGBTQ+ in employment, housing, and public accommodations (ACLU, n.d.). In addition, many of us who grew up in a religious household will be discriminated against by the members of the said religious community, sometimes even by our own families. This can lead to many emotional and psychological issues, including depression, anxiety, social isolation, illicit drug use, and emotional dysregulation (American Psychiatric

Association, n.d.). Some people who go through this might even end up suicidal.

Medical issues and disparities in health care access might also be overlooked by those in the LGBTQ+ community. For example, it has been reported that many transgender people cannot get the type of care they need when it comes to hormone replacement therapy or gender-affirming surgeries. Part of this is due to a lack of information and study on transgender people and discrimination against them in the medical community (American Psychiatric Association, n.d.). This lack of healthcare can lead to suicide within the transgender community.

The lack of understanding of the struggles of LGBTQ+ youth and adults contribute to many disparities. This includes the distribution of justice, liberty, and general welfare that are supposed to be provided for all in our society. As I learned more about myself, including strengthening my foundation to face the next day's challenges, I realized that as a gay man, I need to thrive amidst these challenges. I realized that I could not change society on my own. However, I can change how I present my narrative to society with a renewed sense of self.

Choosing to Change Your Narrative

It could seem hard to overcome the hatred and persecution of people like us when there are so many odds against us. Accepting oneself and the world we live in is a necessary step in learning how to live in the present. It's crucial to learn to accept and love yourself in the face of people who would hurt you since you might not be accepted by those around you. You would also do well to acknowledge the flaws in others around you.

Think of yourself as a child. The world around you is fresh and new. You have not yet learned enough about society to judge what you observe. Instead, you simply see the world as it is, and for what it is. A rock is simply a rock, not necessarily a valuable diamond. A flower is simply a flower, not a rose that many see as the symbol of love. This child can be thought of as the Higher Self and is a state that we should all attempt to achieve (Stevens, 2021).

Unfortunately, society quickly creates a sort of limiting voice within us. This voice is created from people constantly telling us that we are wrong, or that we are sinful. This voice is created from all of the negativity that is pushed into us from an early age; as we grow, so does it, and it becomes an anchor within our own heads.

To begin the process of self-acceptance, you must discover the origin of that inner, limiting voice. It is important to challenge the voice, to think for yourself rather than allowing society's hold on you to guide you. You must rid yourself of that limiting voice, instead creating one for yourself.

For example, it was not just one voice, but rather the voices of many that told me that my sexual orientation is a choice. As an adult, those voices have lingered at the back of my mind. However, I chose to silence those voices and be true to who I am, what I feel, how I see myself, and how I love, care, and think. I eliminated the painful messages from taking part in my daily journey. Only then, was I able to begin writing my life story the way that it should have been written based on who I truly am and not a vision, expectation, mold, or hope of what I should be.

I decided to share my story as a gay man in full transparency rather than viewing myself through the lens of some notion of who I should be. Young people who face systemic oppression have the chance to develop personally and question prevailing narratives by doing this (Wagman et al., 2018). I wish I had understood this when I was a teenager. I wish I had a more vital understanding of who I was and wasn't, rather than being constrained by a conviction that I fervently believed would alter my essence. But now is my time, and you could choose it to be your time too!

According to one study, people who face various forms of discrimination and oppression are frequently silenced by the spread of false narratives rather than information validated through factual checking. Removing the right to challenge unfounded declarations and social assumptions also silence our authentic, lived experience (Wagaman et al., 2018). Before we can prove ourselves or tell our own stories, there are people out there who would tell them for us. Instead of seeing people as individuals, society lumps us and our stories into generalized groups.

We are expected to participate in these groups in a particular way and to share the same narrative as the people we have been partnered with. Stereotypes are developed and cultivated there. Instead of paying attention to those who belong to these social groups, society is willing to accept these lies and false narratives.

Breaking away from the pre-written narrative is one of the most important things that you as an individual can do. You must live a life that reflects who you are, rather than what those around you assume you to be based on your sexual orientation or your gender identity.

Living a Life That Reflects the Real You

Acknowledging that you have a rightful place in society and accepting yourself fully and wholeheartedly is what you deserve. This is something that we all must fully realize before we can be truly happy and at peace with ourselves.

Because of the internal battles I had to win, it took me a long time to honestly believe in this approach. I mistakenly thought that as long as I remained to myself, I could have a complete life, but that is not truly enjoying it. Being proud of your background and experiences allows you to live a fulfilled life that is true to who you are. It's not about conforming to what society expects but about feeling free to live without fear of being judged or out of place.

There are many people out there who are attempting to reclaim some of these negative words in order to turn them into a positive. For many, many years, the term 'queer' was thought of as an insult. In the modern climate of the LBGTQ+ community; however, it has been turned into a qualifying word—a word with power that no longer can be considered insulting.

However, being different is something we are trained to avoid from a young age. It is wrong to be unique. We are, somehow, fundamentally incorrect if we identify as LGBTQ+. They are considered insults because of this. Our reputation as the "black sheep" stems from this. Our culture has taught us to be ashamed of who we are. And people outside of our community view us as something to ridicule, reject or accept cautiously with conditions.

Because of this, there are a lot of people that despise us simply for being alive. This explains why violent crimes are committed on LGBTQ+ people every day. Fear would only fuel that hatred and rage if we lived in it. To challenge the prejudices held about ourselves by others, we must first embrace and love ourselves. We must demonstrate to the oppressive element of society that we are not frightened, despite how challenging, terrible, and painful it is. This action starts with putting on the armor of our true selves every day, which stands for the complete acceptance of who we are as distinctive and resilient individuals.

Accepting Yourself and Being at Peace

Our deepest desires are to be at peace with ourselves. Then we can unleash our actual selves upon the world. However, being LGBTQ+ presents additional burdens that heterosexuals might not experience. As we previously discussed, when additional factors like religion, culture, race, peer pressure, social media, etc. are considered, it can seem as though the obstacles to obtaining inner peace are insurmountable. You need to keep in mind that it can take some time for you to embrace who you are. You've already taken important steps to position yourself to maintain this momentum if you think back to where you started a chapter ago.

What does it mean to be at peace with yourself? This can be a difficult question to answer. An article from the Kentucky Counseling Center's website (2021) puts it this way,

> Inner peace is defined as the state of physical and spiritual calm despite many stressors. Finding your peace of mind means attaining happiness, contentment, and bliss no matter how difficult things get in your life. Finding happiness and inner peace does not depend on a problem-free life or the absence of conflict because we all go through challenges in our lives.

By finding your inner peace—whatever that means for you as an individual—you will find that you are more open to new experiences, and you are more intune with your own personal needs and wellbeing. By finding inner peace, you will be able to also find self-acceptance.

One of the things that you need to remind yourself of is that self-acceptance may take some time to happen. If you look back from when you started a chapter ago, you have already made significant steps in setting yourself up to keep this momentum going. Being at peace begins with the "...moment you choose not to allow another person or event to control your emotions" (The Joy

Within, 2019). Many people believe that inner peace means that they have to be extremely spiritual or religious, or that they tend to keep themselves separated from the world's challenges or issues (The Joy Within, 2019). This is not true at all; rather, having inner peace simply means that you no longer allow others to dictate to you how to live your life. You are in control of yourself, who you are and who you want to be. You are at peace with this.

Part of finding that inner peace means coming to terms with your sexual orientation or your gender identity. Allowing yourself to be at ease with who you are, and not allowing outside forces to attempt to change you–that is inner peace. Remember that self-acceptance is not the same as self-esteem (Seltzer, 2008). While you might have high self-esteem–you see yourself as good looking, smart, etc.—that is not the same as accepting yourself. Self-acceptance comes more from an inner light, loving yourself for both your talents and your flaws, rather than casting away your flaws all together. Self-esteem is important; however, self-acceptance could be seen as most important in your journey of self-growth and discovery.

Self-acceptance is unconditional, and self-compassion is essential. Many of our harmful behaviors are linked to psychological defenses, according to Leon Seltzer, Ph.D. He recognized these points as significant stopping points in his paper (Seltzer, 2008). When the mind or body reaches a certain point, it can no longer defend itself. The defenses deteriorate until there is nothing left to give. Letting go of the need to protect yourself all the time opens the door to more positive behaviors, such as kindness toward oneself and others, a sense of serenity, clarity, purpose, and joy. The possibilities are unlimited.

To finally accept yourself for who you are, flaws and all—that is a thing of beauty. Then, finally, say that you love yourself for who you are, all of who you are—that is self-acceptance. That is what is essential.

Chapter 3:

Healing Through Self-

Compassion

Self-compassion is just as important as inner peace and self-acceptance. Kristen Neff wrote, "Self-compassion is an emotionally positive self-attitude that should protect against the negative consequences of self-judgment, isolation, and rumination (such as depression)" (Neff, 2003). Basically, self-acceptance is learning to accept who you are as a person. Self-compassion is allowing yourself to love yourself, even if there are things about you that you do not like. Instead of wallowing in self-hate or self-pity, self-compassion allows you to look at the good parts of yourself without beating yourself up for the bad parts of yourself.

Remember that forgiving yourself is crucial, if not vital. Keep in mind that embracing yourself—flaws and all—is essential. Even when it seems difficult, remember to be kind to yourself and encourage yourself. On your path to accepting who you are, self-compassion is a crucial component. You are powerful. You are cherished. You have good character unaffected by your sexual orientation or gender identity. Over everything, you are human, and you deserve compassion. You deserve to be seen, heard, loved, and understood. You must see yourself, listen to yourself, love yourself, and understand yourself.

It's Okay to Leave it in the Past

You have come a long way to get to this point, where healing from pain and suffering might be possible. The most crucial part is that you have moved on and added many steps to your 1,000-mile journey. Even if you have lost track of your progress, one thing is for sure—you are no longer where you were when you left the starting line.

The reassurance that you were born with unique handprints and qualities, like any other human being, was your rightful entry to claim your place in this world. However, now that you've gathered strength, courage, and earned entitlement to accept your true self, we cannot forget the struggles and emotional battles that left scars inside of you. I realize that this trauma does not go away after self-acceptance. It lingers. I still went through some fear, self-doubt, feelings of disappointment, and shame. What's different now is that I am on a path to— hopefully—remove those tags one by one.

It might feel difficult to leave that pain in the past. It feels so fresh sometimes, like a wound reopening under the bandages. These wounds will scar, eventually, though it takes time. Everything takes time. What is essential to do is to push through, to remind yourself that those injuries will heal and scar over. You will wear them like a badge of honor; they are proof of your past.

The human experience is made up of the past, the present, and the future. For many, it is difficult to leave that pain in the past where it belongs. It would help if you pushed through that, however. You must keep going and live in the present. Of course, it's okay to think back on previous unpleasant experiences, but try not to let them block your vision as you step forward. For many, these scars I am discussing are symbolic. However, some people carry very real physical scars from their pasts. Some of us were mentally abused, while others were physically abused. It is tough to let that kind of pain go. But, to be kind to yourself and to move forward, you must accept that these things happened to you. You have to recognize that you were harmed, injured, and heartbroken by someone.

It is difficult and might feel impossible, but what was done to you does not define you. Though you were hurt and was left their marks, they do not get to control your future. They never possessed that power to begin with.

Leave them in the past; that's perfectly fine. You'll experience a new sense of freedom after you put these thoughts, feelings, and unbearable emotions in the past, a release from such harm, unpleasant feelings, and injuries. That is incredibly powerful all by itself. Again, you must also permit yourself to practice self-compassion and self-care. This will pave the way for an abundance of positive emotions in the future.

Be Kind to Yourself

What does it mean to be kind? What does it mean to be kind to yourself? Kindness is doing a service or action for another being without the thought of reward (Miller, 2019). This means that you do something nice for someone, something to help them or aid them in their lives, without wanting some kind of reward or praise in return. You do it simply to do it. A wise couple once said, "When we are mindful of our struggles and respond to ourselves with compassion, kindness, and support in times of difficulty, things start to change. We can learn to embrace ourselves and our lives, despite inner and outer imperfections, and provide ourselves with the strength needed to thrive" (Neff & Germer, 2019).

Though it is difficult at times, self-compassion can and will lead to a better understanding of who you are and a better overall outlook on life. Compassion is the grace you would give to someone else who is having a difficult time. But in self-compassion, you give this grace to yourself. It is about making yourself feel good, about allowing yourself to make mistakes or be angry, and knowing that those feelings and moments are allowed and natural.

Consider this: if you and a friend were hiking and your friend slipped off the trail, causing an ankle injury, you wouldn't be angry with them. Instead, you understand that it was a mistake, that your friend was hurt, and needed consolation. Let's pretend you accidentally left the trail now. Would you start criticizing yourself for falling right away? This is where you need to exercise kindness to yourself. Apply the empathy and comfort you would extend to a friend in a similar situation to yourself.

Feeling good for once doesn't mean that you have escaped the world's harsh realities. The world can still be cruel. However, you can now take in sips of air because you have empowered yourself to do so. You don't have to drown in negativity. You no longer feel invalidated, a nuisance, or like someone to be stared at. Instead, when things are hard to understand, you have the bravery to assert that you have the same, equal right to consider another person and attempt to understand their point of view.

Lifting Yourself Up

One of the hardest things to do when you're down is to find an ounce of energy to make it worth getting back up—even if you only fall back down again. How we wish we could wave a magic wand, and then suddenly, everyone likes or agrees with us! In the LGBTQ+ world, kindness from others is a treasured gem. So many people will try to put us down simply because we do not fit within their comfort levels. That is a significant moment when someone comes along and loves us with no strings attached or even allows us to exist within their space. Accepting who we are is undoubtedly a treasure we want to hoard. Instead of understanding the complex journey LGBTQ+ people go through, people exercise cruelty and impose hurt. We wish that people would be at least kind about their struggles when they don't understand anything about it. Better yet—leave us alone!

Just as you have come this far in your journey, you have always had the power to lift yourself up when challenging times happen to you. May I remind you that this is a journey of a lifetime? You don't just give up at the first sign of difficulty. Moreover, you take the fall, but you give yourself no other option but to stand up as quickly as possible. In simple terms: you've got this! This is your journey. This is your time to shine. You are a human being who deserves to exist and live your life to the fullest.

Take a step back when you feel down or hurt or at the end of your rope. Take a deep breath. Count to ten–and then unleash a wave of self-compassion on yourself. Lift yourself up and practice lifting yourself up as often as you need to. This can be simply allowing yourself a compliment, like telling yourself your hair looks perfect today or that your new shirt looks fantastic on you. Maybe it's something more personal, like complimenting yourself on how deep your voice has gotten or how high you can make it if you are trans. Perhaps, it's something as simple as congratulating yourself for remembering to eat breakfast.

Lift yourself up by focusing on the good things in your life. Don't focus on the bad. When something terrible happens, allow it to crash on you like a wave–feel it at that moment–and then let it go back out to sea. Understand why it felt terrible, understand that it impacted you, breathe, and let it go. Once it's gone, allow yourself to feel something good. Allow yourself to feel the sun on your skin or the gentle spray of the ocean against your back. Allow yourself happiness; no one else will do that for you.

Pat Yourself on the Back: You Are Courageous

Accepting yourself as LGBTQ+ is perhaps one of the hardest emotional journeys you'll ever take. For some, this is easy; those who have had very understanding and loving families are lucky. However, for those who do not have that kind of support, coming out of the proverbial closet can feel like walking into a den of hungry lions. Sometimes it is unsafe to come out. Your choice and personal act of living courageously as an authentic human being is unthinkable, knowing that it will expose you to hatred, ignorance, and cruelty.

Guess what, though? You did it anyway! Your strength to put it all on the line to live your true self is the measure only the strong-hearted are willing to take. What does courage mean, though? It might be different for everyone. Courage might be speaking up for something you believe in—something that you believe is right. It might be waking up every morning and getting out of bed. It might be as simple as existing in a world that would rather you didn't. Technically speaking, courage is, "...the ability to do something difficult even when there's risk. Courageous people do and say what they think is right despite opposition" (Common Sense Media, 2020).

Courage might make you feel sick to your stomach, but you continue with what you believe is right. Being courageous does not mean that you are free from fear either; plenty of courageous individuals felt fear, surely, even as they championed for what they believed in. To be courageous requires strong self-advocacy. This means that you communicate your needs, understand those needs, and know what kind of help you have to find in order to meet those needs (Lee, 2014).

For those of us who are LGBTQ+, self-advocacy might look like requesting gender-neutral bathrooms in our schools and workplaces or joining the Gay/Straight Alliance Club at our college. It might also look like creating a safe space for LGBTQ+ people to talk–as easily as creating a chat room online, or a server where people can discuss ways to stay safe, come out, etc. You are not alone. Please remember that. There is a massive list of LGBTQ+ people before you who have paved the way for where you are now.

It might be easy to think that you are alone, but you are not. You never were. Along with Marsha P. Johnson was Sylvia Rivera, a Latina trans woman and activist (Selby, 2018). The two founded STAR (Street Transvestite Action Revolutionaries), which is an organization that has provided housing and resources for homeless LGBTQ+ youths within New York City (Selby, 2018). She was well known for her courageous attitude—and she was even reported to have tried to sneak into a room where NYC council members were debating a bill about gay rights (Selby, 2018).

It is important to remember that, had these two women not come out as transgender and queer, that we probably would not have the rights that we do today. They were the women that really spearheaded the LGBTQ+ rights movement. In the 1970's, Harvey Milk was the first openly homosexual politician (Selby, 2018). During this short tenure, Milk pushed for equal rights for gays and lesbians–a bill that would pass with only one vote against it (Selby, 2018). Unfortunately, for his advocacy, Milk was assassinated in 1978. Still, his legacy lives on, and in 2009, Milk's birthday was designated as a day of recognition for his life's work (Selby, 2018).

Society might have told these three individuals that they were wrong, that they were sinners. They were punished for their crimes of simply being themselves—and yet, without them, without their advocacy, we would not be here today, in the open, allowed to be ourselves. There is plenty of work yet to be done, but because of great leaders like them, we at least do not have to start at the rock bottom.

Just remember–you are not wrong. No, you are not built wrong, made sinister, or born wrong.

Everything about you is very, extraordinarily, brilliantly right. Living your life to the fullest, living your life out of the closet–that takes a lot of courage.

Chapter 4:

It's Okay to Let Go of

What Others Think

Focusing on being comfortable with your unhidden skin and your new self-acceptance is essential. So let's explore your new, unhidden life and what that means for your journey forward.

By this point in your journey, you may likely already be self-accepting—but what about society? What about the other communities you belong to, like your family and your friend groups? Will how they look at you change when you come out to them? These are legitimate fears. Let's look at how those around you might react to learning that you are LGBTQ+.

Reactions From Family and Friends

Our families provided a safe space when we were born, and for some or most of us, as we grew older. Undoing this sacred bond is not necessarily the goal. However, you must understand that not all families are accepting. If you are in one with full-on and unconditional love for you, consider yourself blessed and lucky. However, for the rest of us who have come out and have gone through the process of self-acceptance may remain unsure of our reactions, know that you are not alone. Like our own journey, our families and friends will probably have to go through a similar journey.

It is crucial to understand that how you generally feel as a person shouldn't be influenced by how individuals around you react. You can no longer let the opinions, attitudes, or deeds of others define who you are as a person. It is not your responsibility if someone you care about chooses to reject you. In this situation, this is not your fault. All you do is exist as a human and live an authentic life. It's challenging to comprehend conditional love. We all deserve, however, to be loved and accepted without conditions. There is no basis for valuing the concept of you as a different individual. With time, loving yourself can fill the holes left behind by those who decided to not provide extended support or care for you. It is difficult to be sure; you will have fewer people to fall back on when you need comfort and help. However, ask yourself: was their comfort or support genuine? If they truly loved you for who you are, then the moment of coming out to them should not have changed their outlook on you. They should have still loved you. Therefore, they would not have cast you away.

Unfortunately, a large portion of the negativity we feel about ourselves results from what individuals around us are thinking or taught to believe. Sadly, we are shamed for belonging to the LGBTQ+ community because of external influences. I don't think that anyone was born to hate homosexuals, trans people, or people from other races or different religious beliefs.

However, we cannot deny that hate exists and can originate from homes, institutions, social networks, and our neighborhoods. Therefore, you will always revisit those negative emotions if you are surrounded by negativity. On the other hand, you will always return to that kind of love if you are surrounded by unconditional love. As difficult as it might be, you need to break away from those that wish to harm you, hurt you, or change you. Your father might claim to love you, for example, but when you come out to him as a trans man, he doesn't love you if he disowns you and calls you horrible names. He only loved your image in his mind; he loved the fictional being in his head that wore your face.

You do not deserve to suffer because others can't accept you. Instead, you deserve to be cherished. A key component of loving yourself is freedom from harmful influences and attitudes. This could mean even though you love your family, preserving yourself as you come to terms with self-acceptance takes priority. You may need to remove yourself from them as safely and thoughtfully as possible to avoid further physical and emotional harm.

Support from LGBTQ+ community organizations is also available. Always surround yourself with those who can keep you safe, affirm who you are, and build you up. The best thing you can do is love, especially if you're not LGBTQ+ but are still open to learning about and supporting people who are. Embrace the person you are trying to help. Listen to them. Tell them you love them and that you accept them. Although you might not fully understand their emotions or the struggles of being LGBTQ+, the most important thing you can offer is your support.

You must understand that many of us end up losing our loved ones when we come out. Though we have existed since the beginning of humankind, many people see us as something new. Religious communities see us as a growing force, having some "gay agenda." This is not true. LGBTQ+ people have become more vocal (Ryan, 2014). We are also more present in the media, from books and movies to video games and television shows. There are gay superheroes in comic books when, before, we were forgotten or the punchline of a joke. There are books about young LGBTQ+ kids coming into their own and learning to love and accept themselves. We are nothing new, but now, we have a voice. And we are going to use it.

Coming Together: Our Allies

As a dramatic assertion of space for LGBTQ people and groups, Pride celebrations in the United States began in the late 1960s and early 1970s. Pride in the modern day has developed into a month-long festival that is highly visible all over the globe. However, Pride as a subjective experience and a way to represent communities is still a complex concept. At Pride events and information you can read online, the role of allies cannot be underestimated. It's because of LGBTQ+ allies that our concerns and perspectives have an opportunity to be heard in areas where such topics may not have been considered.

As I was thinking about allyship in the LGBTQ+ sense, I automatically equated the thought to "warfare." It's a strong word for sure but given the tensions and division our society is facing today with LGBTQ+ issues and acceptance at the center, any open space for communication and exchange of ideas has become a battlefield. The only difference in my opinion is that in this warfare, nobody gets to declare an all-encompassing victory.

Rather, the victory is won when hearts are changed. LGBTQ+ allies are our saving grace because they are able to share their experiences and perspectives as seen in their process of changing how they see LGBTQ+ people. Our allies are our community. They become the eyes and ears of advocating to others for compassion and kindness on our behalf. I consider them precious gifts in this time of difficulty and in our fight for equality.

Being an ally indicates that you want our voices to be heard. You want to see and hear us, which is a wonderful gift. Allyship is to not speak for us but to speak about us as equals in society. We can gradually but steadily make the world a safer place for the children who will follow us by changing the way people view LGBTQ+ individuals. The University College London in its student website, listed seven things you can do as an LGBTQ+ ally. We all have heard that allies need to be ready to listen and be educated on the plight of LGBTQ+ persons. However, checking your privilege is one that caught my attention. According to the post, whether it is due to race, class, education, being cisgender, being physically fit, or straight, most people (including those who identify as LGBTQ+) enjoy some form of privilege. Being affluent does not negate the fact that you have experienced your fair share of hardships. Just put, it means that some things you will never have to consider or worry about simply because of how you were born.

You can better relate to persecuted or isolated groups if you know your privileges (Carroll, 2021).

The post said one should not take your friend's, coworker's, or roommate's sexual orientation for granted. Don't assume someone's pronouns or gender. LGBTQ+ persons don't have a specific appearance. Their sexual orientation is not defined by their present or former partners (yes, bisexuals, pansexuals, and queer people exist). Someone close to you might need assistance; if you don't assume anything, you'll offer them the room they require to be themselves and open up to you when the time is right (Carroll, 2021). The most potent takeaway from that piece was to consider allyship as an action rather than a label. I was astounded by how much of this spoke to me after reading it. While we must be grateful for whatever support we get, having an ally also comes with obligations. Furthermore, even if it is simple to refer to oneself as an ally, this is insufficient. There will always be oppression. If you want to be a successful ally, you must be prepared to defend LGBTQ+ people from prejudice and continuously promote LGBTQ+ rights. Inform your loved ones, friends, and coworkers that you are an ally and find anti-LGBTQ+ comments and jokes hurtful. True acceptance and respect require the cooperation of every member of society, and your open and steadfast support will hopefully serve as an inspiration to others (Carroll, 2021).

Allies may develop their identities due to seeing something that, in their eyes, did not feel or seem right. Then, they acted upon their guts to stop the event even though they were unaware of the circumstances. For example, breaking up a quarrel between siblings, youngsters, or kids at the playground could suffice. You can learn to support and love your LGBTQ+ child or a person in general for who they are, even if you do not think being LGBTQ+ is a positive thing. Children are particularly at risk in these situations. If you reject your child, you increase their chance of self-harm or suicide and their likelihood of developing depression or drug addiction (Option B, 2009). On the other hand, families who accept their LGBTQ+ children are likely to have healthier kids with a lower incidence of depression or self-harm (Option B, 2009).

Speak up! There are a variety of reasons why individuals choose not to object when they hear inappropriate phrases like "that's so gay." People may find it embarrassing, unsure of how to respond, or unwilling to aggravate the circumstance. But a word can sting. Speaking up informs others, makes them aware that their statements are unacceptable, and could even inspire others to speak up on their own. Furthermore, you have the power to influence future behavior. This is strong. Sincerity is crucial. Be truthful if your friends, family members, and coworkers are LGBTQ+ and agree to your discussing it. People frequently discuss their gender identification or sexual preference. Kindly lend a hand to the LGBTQ+ community. Remember, showing your support online or by joining an LGBTQ+ group, or an organization managed by students, counts as showing your support. Allies are true supporters of the LGBTQ+ community. They have the potential to be strong advocates for LGBTQ+ equality who not only make it easier for LGBTQ+ individuals to come out, but who also educate others on the value of justice and equality for everyone.

LGBTQ+ people can lead perfectly happy, normal lives. If your child has just come out to you, you need to remember that they are still your child. They are the same person they were before they came out to you. Maybe they feel a little lighter, having shed this burden of coming out to you, but they are still that same person that you have loved and cherished. The only difference now is that they are sharing more of themselves with you; now, you can see more of who they truly are. This isn't a curse, it's a blessing. Also keep in mind that disagreements occasionally are acceptable and good!

Focus on the Important Stuff

At this point, you have had a lot to think about. Getting acquainted with your new self is a task in and of itself. You are still the same person, yet you have a new outlook, a different level of self-confidence, and a renewed hope that life will be better if you choose to make it happen. What others think of you should be far from the essential things you still need to work on. You didn't get this far to return to where you started. Like a marathon, you'll get used to the daily workout of putting yourself at the forefront of everything. Just because you have achieved self-acceptance does not mean you are already done. As we mentioned earlier, getting through the processes in this book is just the beginning. It is your life after reading this book that matters.

You have a bright future ahead of you. Thinking about the numerous options for forging your new route, picking your story, and concentrating on the correct things should be an exciting time. We can strive to develop ways where we can imagine what our ideal future state looks like as it is impossible to reliably foretell the future, unless you have the gift. A word that comes to me is "visioning. " Your persistence, confidence, and trust in your abilities and basic beliefs will be put to the test throughout the period after self-acceptance. Trying to picture who you will be in the future could be difficult—I experienced the same issue. Without the support of my loving husband, I likely would have felt so vulnerable and alone that visioning would have been the last thing on my mind.

The process of visioning serves as a steady source of guidance or illumination for the ideal future while you negotiate these uncharted waters. By linking actual components or designs, rather than just daydreaming about them, you may continue constructing them and watching them come to pass. If you think of a lighthouse, we rarely go there immediately; instead, we sail towards it to pass it on our way somewhere else. It is not the goal to create a hard vision and spend a lifetime working to make it a reality.

There can be challenges, and the objective might take on a different shape as we get closer to completing what we had intended. However, we can be certain that we are moving in the right direction by employing visioning (Wahl, 2017). One of the things that can really slow down this process is overthinking about what others might think of you. So, how can you stop worrying about what other people think? How can you prevent their thoughts and actions from impacting your journey? It might seem like a difficult task, but it is one that you need to familiarize yourself with to continue onward.

When we depend too heavily on the opinions of others and deem their approval necessary to our success, we run into issues. Our lives start to be tailored to suit other people's needs. When we give up control and let others' opinions determine how we are perceived, we lose sight of who we really are. The only reality we can see is how we believe others' view of us (Daskal, 2016). Then, how can we concentrate on what ought to be our primary concern? How can we block out the unfavorable opinions of those around us? How do we assess ourselves and live our lives?

Simply put, you must concentrate on what is crucial. Keep to your own lane; after all, most individuals do so. Even though you could feel like everyone is watching you. So, based on that thought, you are evaluating yourself. Most of your vicinity are preoccupied with attending to themselves and their behavior (Daskal, 2016). They criticize themselves just as harshly as you do because they are terrified of being evaluated. Also, keep in mind that you can't please everyone. People will evaluate you according to their preconceived notions. Because everyone has their own set of rules to live by, what is appropriate for one person may not be for another. So pay more attention to what is correct for you than what other people believe is appropriate.

Be sure to focus your attention on an exact period as well. Consider the present moment instead of the past or future. Put your attention on what you are doing, where you are going, and what you want rather than on how you could have changed things in the past. Aim to maintain your sense of reality by using these approaches. Consider yourself and what is best for you instead of focusing on making everyone else happy: past, or present.

Finally, remember that it is your life. You get one life to live–right here, right now. You need to live that life to the best of your abilities. If you constantly focus on pleasing everyone else or on keeping everyone happy with you, you are restraining yourself from living your full and uninhibited life. You're living a life others want you to live. You will never find your own happiness that way. You must be a little self-centered for this

The best thing you could do is surround yourself with positive people and situations. What is appropriate for someone else and what they desire for you may not be what is best for you. Instead of concentrating on what's best for others around you, think about what's best for you. This will help you discover happiness in your own way. To appease the people around you, avoid attempting to change yourself or what you are. Bust that stereotype. Be the person you want to be and the real you and unravel your skin. As you continue reading the next few paragraphs, keep in mind that you have so much important stuff to prioritize and while opinions of others cannot be eliminated, your priority is to make that vision of a fulfilled and authentic life your reality.

Be Aware of Certain Triggers

In my own journey, there have been times when certain memories of the past gave me goosebumps and an overwhelming sense of worry as if I was brought back to the same situation. An emotional trigger for me is when I watch shows or movies where there are scenes of name-calling a gay character. The effect on me is so diminishing as I was called names as a young kid because I was effeminate, or I hung out with girls more.

Even when I was in my freshman year of college, a former high school classmate a year ahead of me called me a "fag" in the native language, even though I was still not ready to be out. The other students who heard it just laughed. The horror and shame I felt were so overwhelming that I just had to smile and dismiss his taunting to try to calm the situation down.

That feeling has stayed with me to this day. What I would like to point out here is that there will be times when you will feel certain emotions, physical symptoms, and reactions that are too familiar during your struggle to self-acceptance. Understand that they will probably not go away permanently. However, there are ways to cope, especially with shame, anxiety, and anger.

Triggers are what create these symptoms, which can be both physical and emotional. Simply put, triggers are anything that elicits strong, negative feelings (Plata, 2018). A place or a word, for instance, might be one of these things. An example of a trigger is recognizing a certain person or even hearing a name. Anything can, in theory, act as a trigger when connected to a bad feeling or memory.

When someone is triggered, they may experience any number of symptoms, including anxiety, nausea, dizziness, chest aches, an elevated heart rate, rage, shaking, and melancholy. These are uncontrollable, involuntary reactions from the person in question. Additionally, there are several trigger categories, including anger, trauma, and anxiety triggers (Plata, 2018). The term "anxiety trigger" refers to a trigger focused on specific emotional anxiety. These induce unnecessary stress and a panicked mood. Such triggers may cause a person to enter the flight-or-fight response state.

Posttraumatic stress disorder (PTSD) is frequently linked to trauma triggers (Plata, 2018). Abuse or traumatic experiences, such as being in a war or being in an abusive relationship can lead to PTSD. When someone becomes irrationally furious for no apparent cause, this is known as an anger trigger. Anything that sets off this reaction, whether it be an item, a circumstance, a person, or a location, can make someone angry (Plata, 2018).

It might be challenging to calm yourself down after being triggered. Some individuals, for instance, require complete removal from the situation. Others must be brought back to their feet by breathing exercises, direct physical touch with a person, a service animal trained for such cases, or both. A trained emotional support animal, such as a cat, might, for instance, settle down on its owner's lap to help them re-establish contact with reality. Here, the cat's weight is a physical reminder of the environment surrounding the person who has been triggered.

The message here is clear: triggers are disabling, and practicing your responses is essential. With that said, we can be more deliberate about addressing our deepest emotional needs or dealing with anything that can threaten us. When we are aware of our triggers, we understand better how we can manage them (Stahlmann & Hagaman, 2019). For our own welfare, it is essential to be conscious of all our feelings, whether they are pleasant or negative. If we want to conquer or avoid our triggers, we must first grasp what they are.

Let's imagine, for example, that your grandfather disowned you after you told him you were bisexual. He wouldn't even look you in the eye and was ferociously upset with you. He used derogatory language against you and came dangerously close to hitting you. Fortunately, your grandma intervened and separated the two of you so that you could safely leave their home. Your traumatic event could cause you to acquire a trigger when you see your grandfather's face. You might now be more sensitive to tall, broad-shouldered males because your grandfather had a similar body type. Perhaps, screaming sets you off. You can better manage your triggers if you know where they originate. You will avoid your granddad if you are aware that he makes you physically react negatively. Suppose you are aware that shouting or yelling sets off your triggers. In that case, you will try to avoid any setting where individuals are screaming or crying.

Of course, there will be circumstances in which you are powerless to control your triggers. For example, there will be moments when others around you begin shouting without consideration for those of us with such a trigger. In that situation, you need to have a method of grounding yourself so that you can go through the incident, through the time when you are triggered, or at the very least until you can get out of the situation. Everyone's definition of it is unique.

For example, breathing exercises are used by some people to maintain their composure. Some people carry an object like a worry stone or fidget spinner to keep themselves occupied while waiting to feel safe. Others, as was mentioned before, can rely on a service or emotional support animal during these difficult periods of their emotional and physical well-being. There might be moments when you have flashbacks to disturbing or intense moments in your life. These might be flashbacks of having gone through abuse or some other kind of violent act. This is linked to PTSD, and it would be a good idea to seek professional help in dealing with these triggers and symptoms.

Whatever the case, being aware and conscious of your triggers is extremely important. By keeping them under control, you will be able to feel more emotionally fulfilled and safe. Make sure that those that are close to you know about your different triggers. This will help them help you when you are triggered, as well as help them to understand and know what to do and not to do. Then, regardless of your pace, you're able to move forward to achieve your goal of self-acceptance.

Being open and honest about the things that trigger you might feel difficult at first. You might feel like you are weak if you admit to these kinds of things. You are strong for putting yourself out there, for admitting that you have things that make you feel emotionally and physically unwell. Just like you have learned how to be honest with yourself about your sexuality or your gender identity, you must also learn how to be honest with yourself and others concerning the things that trigger you.

Remember, being triggered is not a sign of weakness. It is a sign of past trauma that still bothers you today. You are stronger when you learn how to deal with that trauma, with those horrible feelings of anxiety, nausea, and so forth. Be proud of yourself for admitting that you have triggers. Be proud of yourself for admitting that you need help.

The Joy of Inclusion

Dr. Brene Brown, who I quoted earlier in the book, said in one of her TEDx talks, "don't walk through the world looking for evidence that you don't belong because you'll always find it." This is a poignant reminder that when we are protecting or advocating for ourselves, we may feel alone and unsure of what we are doing. You have the power to reject actions by those who try to diminish your lived experience. But think about this for a second.

Instead of finding reasons why you couldn't stand with confidence, why you couldn't take your place at the table, or why being LGBTQ+ will make it extremely difficult to belong. Just remember that many others have gone through a similar experience before us. Nevertheless, they took their seats at the table, and they survived. One can only feel valued, respected, and supported in an inclusive environment. It means stressing everyone's needs and ensuring the best circumstances are offered so they can realize their most significant potential.

For a diverse community to be supported, a society's culture, customs, and relationships should all encourage inclusivity. Creating an inclusive community culture and environment allows one to respect, value, and utilize each person's abilities, knowledge, and perspectives. It also strengthens ties within the community and promotes cooperation, adaptability, and fairness. To make it clearer, inclusion is a system of behaviors (culture) that fosters a sense of value among a group of people for their distinctive backgrounds and skill sets.

Feeling included gives one a sense of belonging (HUD, 2022).

The idea of "visioning" was covered in the previous chapter. But the description provided above borders on wishful thinking.. That story seems more like a vision than a description of reality. The ability to put yourself in the best possible situations in life to fulfill your potential is one of the most essential advantages of self-acceptance. You made the decision to act. While we all long for a society where tolerance and understanding of the variations in individuals, cultures, customs, and relationships are the standard, we are not there yet. That is the microcosm, which we hope spreads globally. But we are alive today and the actions we take to strengthen ourselves matter.

So, where inclusivity exists, we must seize it and celebrate it. This is what it means to be inclusive when you are a part of a group with a unique history. That group is what we are. The LGBTQ+ community. There is strength in our inclusiveness even though we are still developing and have flaws. The delight of inclusion comes with this power. You've embraced a group of admirable people now that you've accepted or in the process of accepting who you really are. We are people who have traveled the same path toward self-acceptance as you have or are now doing. We have similar life experiences.

You may have momentarily lost touch with your immediate family or friends due to your life-altering path toward self-acceptance, whether voluntarily or not. I just wanted to let you know that LGBTQ+ communities in your town, city, state, and all across the world are affirming, positive, and supportive. It's powerful to consider this. You've also given yourself permission to be brave by joining a network that will seek to change how LGBTQ+ people live their lives in the years to come. Our collective stories are a component of this power, as was mentioned in the earlier chapters. This gives me a sense of excitement, security, and hope.

If you don't know where to begin, looking for a community organization online is a great way to start. Numerous social media groups are available for LGBTQ+ people to communicate. Furthermore, you can report anyone who tries to intimidate or harass you because these communities are equipped to get you to the resources you may need. In these meetings, LGBTQ+ individuals are expected to feel safe.

LGBTQ+ Allyship in Action

These days, there are numerous LGBTQ+ support and celebration clubs for after-school events in high schools and middle schools. If you're an adult looking for LGBTQ+ parent groups, volunteering to assist with these organizations is a great way to find them while also supporting the future members of our communities. In addition, an excellent approach to meeting new people and getting your voice heard if you're younger is to join one of these organizations while you're still in school. There are clubs or organizations like these at specific colleges as well. Many communities and faith-based organizations are now learning to support LGBTQ+ individuals. This implies that there might be a gathering place for LGBTQ+ individuals in your church or other institution of worship.

Indications that a restaurant or store is a safe area for the LGBTQ+ community are common in locally owned companies. For example, the front door may have rainbow flags or stickers, and there may be "love is love" or "no hatred" signs. These locations provide a secure, welcoming environment where people of all sexual orientations and gender identities can congregate or relax with a cup of coffee. Some of these companies might be comic bookstores or game stores. They traditionally set aside space to play games or different card games on certain evenings of the week. Meeting LGBTQ+ people and allies in your neighborhood can be accomplished through such activities.

LGBTQ+ allies are a separate group of people ready to accept and support you, as a person, first and your essence as an individual. While an LGBTQ+ ally's role can vary, in general, these people are ardent advocates who are aware of the problems the community is facing and are eager to learn more about them. They also offer a secure setting for LGBTQ+ people to talk about issues they are having at work or more broadly in life. Allies work to increase communication, empathy, the reach of their support outside the LGBTQ+ community, and the chance for others to learn about the community's problems. Since it extends public support at Pride events and offers private spaces for conversation, the traditional ally stance is very advantageous. Alternative tactics, however, can encourage more significant support and engagement.

The role of allies is to encourage more collaboration, inspire empathy, ensure support outside the LGBTQ+ community, and provide the opportunity for people to learn about issues affecting the group." The traditional ally role is particularly advantageous since it provides places where people may talk in safety and extends visible support at Pride events. Therefore, leaders must have open discussions so that community members may see that they are encouraged and have a voice (Lataille & O'Neill, 2022).

Allies demonstrate their love and support for the LGBTQ+ community in this way. Furthermore, they frequently represent us when people focus on us. However, this arrangement is less than ideal since LGBTQ+ people should be heard about issues affecting our community, even though having allies to support us is positive. Therefore, leaders must engage in honest dialogues to reassure community members that they are kept in an environment where they can excel, and their voices heard. The importance of allies to our mental health as a support system cannot be overstated. Having someone there for you is a powerful and comforting emotion, regardless of where you land on the sexual orientation or gender identity continuum. It's like always having someone looking out for your best interests and ensuring your safety.

Welcoming the New You

So, what does it mean to welcome the "new you"? The phrase "new you" refers to your recent life-changing transformation. Without being dramatic, you have begun the process of your own evolution. It can be referred to as awakening, changeover, modification, etc. Only you know what has changed in your feelings, thoughts or perception of yourself. This is a historical moment brought about by your determination to live because life is worth living for. This is no longer the part of your life you will fight. You've accepted your true self and already won half the battle. Remember this day when you truly, unequivocally, and completely received yourself as an LGBTQ+ person.

As part of the joy of inclusion, we discussed the sense of belonging. This is the time to experience that your newfound sense of belonging to a group of people can boost your motivation, health, and happiness. Relationships with people going through similar things provide comfort because they show you that you are not alone. If you don't already have one, you should look for one, even if it's uncomfortable for you. Try to communicate with and interact with others. As a result, you'll notice that your life is richer and that you've improved as a person. Remember that we all have something in common, but our perspectives differ. These diverse perspectives enable areas to be strengthened. These distinct perspectives allow us to support areas of our lives that require it the most.

A community is necessary for you to function as an individual. Never lose sight of the fact that our species only survives in settings where people help one another. The presence of a warm community is like receiving a priceless gift. It's impossible to estimate how much you can give back or pay forward once you've received the rewards. But one thing is for sure. You would want everyone following you on the same path to have the same experience.

A community treats someone in that way. You flourish in it and gracefully transform while maintaining your uniqueness and freedom of choice. Community is a way of life, not a location. You leave the experience feeling bold and assured. Self-confidence and general well-being are greatly enhanced by community involvement. Even if you are an introvert, you should learn to value the benefits of socializing. Belonging to a community provides resources, a sense of belonging, opportunities to try new things or see things from different perspectives, help, and support one another, and strength in numbers (Catherine, 2019).

In addition, we can experience more growth and success with others than with ourselves. Communities are essential to our survival in every way. We gather with our friends, family, coworkers, neighborhoods, and other communities. We find community in our various interest groups and sports teams, the musicians we admire, and even the foods we eat. A sense of belonging binds us all together. We sometimes feel like we're a part of something bigger than ourselves when we're a part of these communities.

As a result, we can increase our level of engagement and support in ways that we would not have been able to otherwise. Finding a community where you fit in and feel at ease is wonderful. You are a member of the LGBTQ+ community simply by your identity, whether you identify as a member or an ally. You've discovered a community of people who share your values and will fight for your rights through online activism or in-person interactions. Community is not just about people who agree on many things, but it is loving people that makes a community. This is a community that honors you. You are most welcome here. You're right at home here.

You will no longer be assessing how different you are from others negatively but rather how much more you can improve and learn from others as an LGBTQ+. When you've found a mentor or a support system, you'll notice an awakening of the best in yourself. It's as if you've returned home. But this time, everyone has been waiting for you to arrive at your chosen moment. Welcome, once more, to the new you!

Chapter 5:

You Are Your Biggest

Responsibility

It gives me great joy to finally acknowledge the path you have already traveled. I hope this book's advice and nuggets of wisdom have enabled you to regain control of the story of your life. Simply put, this means expressing your narrative genuinely that reflects your own growth. In a way, maintaining yourself each day is a commitment on your part. "I am not what happened to me," eminent psychologist Carl Jung once said. "I become what I decide to become," he concluded. This is a strong assertion that exudes force, will, and determination. Yet, it wasn't an easy trip for any of us to reach self-acceptance. As a result, sustaining this momentum is more important than ever. Taking care of one of life's most considerable obligations is more important than ever. Ourselves.

We have covered a wide range of topics in this book. First, consider what you've learned considering the present situation. Then, take a moment to reflect on where you started. You were a different person back then, even though you were still yourself. Possibly more reclusive. Perhaps, you lacked self-confidence or were fearful of the future. You must think it's ludicrous at this moment. But, given that you have evolved into the person you were always meant to be, you may look back and see progress that was probably unimaginable then.

Again, be gentle with yourself and your history. Be thankful that you arrived at this precise moment unscathed and still alive. Recognizing your starting point and current state is vital. There is a saying, "Don't forget where you came from but never lose sight of where you are going." Keep in mind that other people are traveling the same path from different backgrounds. The exact efforts you just took to become the best version of yourself are also being taken by many others with varying degrees of burdens to carry.

Even though we've talked a lot about responsibility and obligation to others, that sense of duty will come at the right time, and you'll be able to accept that challenge. For the time being, take a deep breath, savor the moments, and keep visioning. Adjust your light as needed to ensure you can see the path ahead. You still have a lot of work ahead of you. Others will notice your resilience in the process. This is unavoidable because your excitement and a new zest for life will be difficult to contain. Joy is something to be shared. It should inspire and even provide a ray of hope to anyone on the verge of losing faith in humanity. Like me, you might even write a book. Share your stories and strengthen the power in all our stories. Focusing on yourself as you meet others allows you to be inspired by them by squeezing every drop of hope that can only reinforce your lifelong journey. These are the effects I hope you notice. Always remember that by simply being the new you, you are providing opportunities for others in the LGBTQ+ community. When many would prefer you to stay hidden, you are changing the world around you simply by being who you are. That is incredibly important and powerful! You are now prepared to emerge from hiding and must do it fervently. You can succeed and become the beautiful person you were meant to be, and I have faith in your capacity to do so.

Nurture Yourself

Through the years, I observed that the more I nurtured myself, the more I valued and loved myself. Of course, no day is ever the same, and every day has the potential to be dreamy and easy. However, the more I appreciated and loved who I've authentically become, the more I made time for myself because it gives me joy.

This lovely self-sustaining cycle was what I needed to help myself. However, it takes mindfulness to exercise this consistently and reap the most benefits from it. Suppose encouraging words were not in abundance in the early years of our development; in that case, it could be challenging to speak to ourselves lovingly. In fact, we probably learned to criticize and neglect ourselves if we were frequently ignored or yelled at. A key component of mindfulness is being present in the present moment, both internally and externally.

It's simple to lose track of what's happening in the world. It's also simple to become disconnected from how our bodies feel. Oftentimes, we find ourselves too deep in our heads, almost robotic and oblivious to how our thoughts influence our emotions and actions. Reconnecting with our bodies and their feelings is a crucial aspect of mindfulness. This entails being aware of the sights, sounds, smells, tastes, and sensations in the present. Simple clues like how a banister feels as we ascend a flight of stairs could be that. Observing our thoughts and feelings as they occur is another crucial aspect of mindfulness (NHS, 2022).

To show gratitude for this new journey you are on, you must nurture yourself. This represents new hope and a renewed way of life. Treat yourself well and with care as if you were a growing tree. You begin as a little sapling that can hardly support itself, but with love and care, you will one day develop into a strong oak tree. You have traveled a thousand miles and made a lot of progress. Although I've repeated this a few times, I can never emphasize enough that you must stop from time to time, look around, and assess your progress for a moment. Today is an excellent day to think about moving forward rather than retreating. The time has come to tell yourself that you are your most essential responsibility. Yes, you! A lifetime is ahead of you, and the past is behind you.

Nurturing yourself can also mean highlighting your new appreciation for life. Practice mindfulness more and acknowledge the subtle changes day by day. For example, acknowledge it when you smile because of a fun memory or when you remember feeling good about yourself, your daily choices, and the decision to surround yourself with those who support you.

In my journey, I have realized that the story has been bittersweet. While celebrating my freedom of sorts from the emotional burdens of feeling judged amidst the smiling faces, I always wondered what could have been. These moments sometimes make me feel like I failed in some way. But I needed to remind myself that decisions are made on both sides in any relationship. People close to you who have decided to reject you and what you represent as an LGBTQ+ person made that choice as well.

I must caution you that this feeling of sadness can manifest as guilt and self-blame, but you cannot overthink it. It is not helpful. Instead, recognize and appreciate the bursts of joy and hope that you now have, living an authentic life. Practice gratitude to yourself, your body, mind, and spirit. Manifest goodness and kindness by encouraging someone who needs it. No matter how big or small, all success deserves to be celebrated. It wasn't simple to achieve self-acceptance in the first place. So—cheers!

Practicing Gratitude

I want to introduce this topic by quoting an unnamed author who said, "Never be a prisoner of your past. It wasn't a life sentence; it was just a lesson." I wanted to share this because sometimes we need a stark, lasting reminder that we might be too hard on ourselves. In the earlier chapters, I discussed the possibility that some of us might need to end our relationships with those we love. We did it to address the root issues that will allow us to start healing and finally accept ourselves. All of us have a deep-seated desire to constantly be kind to everyone. In this world that's filled with all of us imperfect people, situations, and surroundings, we had to decide on many significant life decisions. We have carried a lifetime of guilt for not knowing our sexuality and for feeling inappropriate about it. Many of us thought of self-hatred and even experienced cruel treatment. Instead of being about sex, homosexuality is about survival. Teens identifying as sexual minorities are five times more likely to be bullied and twice as likely to commit suicide. It is estimated that 29% of LGBTQ+ teenagers have made suicide attempts. As an author, I consider it an honor and a privilege that you are reading this book. So that you would understand that you are no longer a prisoner of your past and that self-acceptance gives genuine hope. I wanted to imply that you accept this message. I am grateful for the possibility that we all have a lifetime to practice gratitude..

What does it mean when we say thank you? This may strike you a bit backward: should I express gratitude to others to feel better about myself? Not necessarily, however, doing so can change the outcome of both your days and enhance your connection. Practicing gratitude or thankfulness and counting your blessings have been shown to improve happiness and reduce depression (Brown & Wong, 2017). Spend a few moments each day expressing thanks to your friends, family, pets, or even inanimate objects that you are just appreciative of.

If necessary, start a gratitude journal and write the many reasons for being alive today. However, telling your friends and family that you appreciate them in person is a beautiful approach. Write short notes to others to show them that you care. Expressing gratitude removes the chains of toxic emotions that keep us from moving forward by unshackling these unhealthy chains in place of the powerful feeling of thankfulness (Brown & Wong, 2017). As in your journey to self-acceptance, this new approach will take time to consistently practice, but there's no day but today to start.

Gratitude also leads to finding a reason to celebrate at every given opportunity because guess what? There are really a million and more reasons to celebrate each day. Getting out of bed each morning is difficult for some, and it is a cause for celebration when someone can place their feet on the ground, stand up, and leave their bedrooms. It is not necessary to throw a lavish celebration of any kind. Just a simple "well done," or perhaps treating yourself to a serving of your preferred caramel swirl ice cream after supper. Try to give yourself credit for any success you have achieved. For example, you might write down "go to work," "have breakfast," "clean the dishes," etc., especially if you've been in such a difficult place for a while. These are the "wins" in your daily life that are worth celebrating.

A Harvard Health Publications article advises, "Write a letter to yourself." Describe a circumstance that made you uncomfortable (a breakup with a lover, a job loss, a poorly received presentation). Without assigning blame to anyone, describe the situation in a letter to yourself. Recognize your emotions. For many, writing serves as a powerful stress relief. You will give yourself time to think about both the positive and the negative by allowing yourself a quiet minute to sit down and write down how you feel. Since writing is considered physical activity, you'll discover that sitting down to write can make you feel less physically stressed.

The bottom line is gratitude has a lasting positive effect on the brain. In the same study by Brown and Wong (2017), they were able to distinguish how people donate money to causes by gratitude versus other motivations, such as feelings of guilt or obligation. They showed those study participants who felt more grateful, reflected brain activity that differed from the brain activity related to guilt and the desire to help a cause.

Using an fMRI scanner, the people who gave more money to a cause showed greater neural sensitivity in the medial prefrontal cortex. This response is associated with learning and decision-making, indicating that more grateful people are also more sensitive to how they express gratitude. A similar conclusion was found in the fMRI scanner for those who wrote gratitude letters. It was observed that they had greater activation in the medial prefrontal cortex when they experienced gratitude. Gratitude changes our priorities to help us mindfully appreciate the things around us.

The Impact of Touch In How We Think

The skin is the largest human organ, composed of many complex nerve systems and receptors that protect the body. It also receives countless external data sent to the brain (Degges-Whlte, 2016). Did you know that getting or giving a hug might lower your blood pressure? Researchers have discovered that a simple embrace or snuggle from someone we love produces the hormone oxytocin which lowers blood pressure, and eases tension (Watson, 2021). So, hug your best buddy or cuddle up with your dog or cat as self-care; you'll feel better for it. For some of us, it may have been a while since we received a wholehearted hug from anyone. Many of us may have been against this practice for traumatic reasons that can cause triggers. I encourage you to consider for a second that a simple hug forms a complex response that warms our hearts and makes us feel better.

As they say, life is a marathon and not a sprint. The journey to self-acceptance is not different. There are many emotions to unpack and taking the time to think is essential. Everyone should take time to remember to do simple things like go outside, take a bath or a shower, or even reflect at the end of the day. Avoid overthinking the wrong stuff and spend more time highlighting where you are today and the wonderful thing about it.

I used to stare into oblivion after many crucial conversations so that my emotions and thinking could be processed simultaneously. The result is my inability to have an internal resolution of what I need to focus on or look forward to the next day. Instead, I carried the same emotions to varying degrees day after day. Thus, the feelings got heavier and more challenging to manage.

It is impossible to live flawlessly every day. You are only human, so you will make mistakes. However, discover how to comprehend and let them go rather than allowing them to harm you. Like how the tide comes in and goes out, it may one day bring lovely shells and the next foul-smelling seaweed. You might discover a pearl before the next wave washes the seaweed away. Most people may find happiness in their surroundings. I once believed that happiness is the sole reason to live and no other motive exists. Otherwise, why put up with pain and hardship? The objective is to find happiness in some form, and I wasn't the only person to believe so. The purpose is a great word to dissect during our thinking time. However, it's also a big word loaded with endless possibilities to overthink and fall into analysis paralysis. We have all heard it before. We all were born for a purpose. But what if that purpose is to be useful in many meaningful ways?

Being useful is a significant purpose of life; enjoyment is merely a result of that (Foroux, 2016). But if you take the time to do modest good deeds every day, it adds to a well-lived life that is important. The last thing I want is to discover that there is no proof of my existence as I lay dying. We can acquire both internal happiness and external usefulness by being kind to others and acting in ways that benefit others rather than ourselves. As we pay it forward to those who are behind us in their journeys to self-acceptance, we can find our version of purposefulness and usefulness in sharing our stories. I shared a lot about the power of our collective experience expressed in storytelling, but this simple act may make a difference with someone who may not be in a good place.

I leave this chapter with an excerpt from Raphael Bob Waksberg's collection of short stories, *Someone Will Love You in All Your Damaged Glory*. He wrote,

> A statue isn't built from the ground up—it's chiseled out of a block of marble—and I often wonder if we aren't likewise shaped by the qualities we lack, outlined by the empty space where the marble used to be. I'll be sitting on a train. I'll be lying awake in bed. I'll be watching a movie; I'll be laughing. And then, all of a sudden, I'll be struck with the paralyzing truth: It's not

what we do that makes us who we are. It's what we don't do that defines us (Waksberg, 2022).

Remind Yourself That You Are Loved

The two most basic human wants are acceptance and love. According to Abraham Maslow, a psychologist who specialized in motivation and need, love and belonging are two of the five basic wants that all people must have to have to live fully. Many people worry that they don't have the sense of community and acceptance they need to fulfill this desire. The inability to receive love from others may make someone feel inadequate or incapable. People who think they are unlovable may feel unable to create boundaries. They tend to compromise their other needs to make these relationships, which is a need that is fundamental in all humans. They may be unaware of their rights to respect the individuals they care about. Remember that no one is intrinsically unlovable (Marschall, 2022). The remnants of the past may keep you from recognizing love when it's in front of you.

The terrifying aspect of coming out for many LGBTQ+ children or adults is telling their parents. You probably think that nothing else matters once your parents are behind you. While accepting your parents is a pivotal point of your journey, you should not underestimate the circle of affirming people you've identified in your road to inclusion discussed in the previous chapter. There are also many others who may not have reached out but are silently ready and willing to provide the love and support you need.

It's time to connect with your friends and others with whom you may not have had a chance to share your story yet. You may still fear rejection, but your strong sense of self will carry you through every day. Remind yourself that you are not the same person you were when this book first began in Chapter 1. Again, support doesn't have to come from your own family alone. Look around you and the network of affirming people you have established or have come to know.

After reading the opening chapter of this book, remind yourself that you have become better, and your situation has shifted for the better. Because of your increased ownership over your narrative, you will be better equipped to handle emotional setbacks. In addition, studies show that LGBTQ+ adolescents with family support grow into happier, healthier adults. Keep in mind that there are both appropriate and inappropriate ways to show love. The right words to speak to us may occasionally elude our loved ones. Direct statements like "I'm sorry" might not always be heard. Open your heart to receiving these quiet expressions of acceptance and love, whether they come in the form of simple gestures like sitting down with you or simple words like "I love you."

Supporting Your LGBTQ+ Loved Ones

Some of the crucial things you can do to support your child or loved one is to love them, so keep that in mind if you are a parent or friend of an LGBTQ+ person reading this book. They must love and trust you enough to want you to be a part of their lives if they have come out to you. They look to you for acceptance and encouragement. To be able to hear their stories is a privilege. Disowning somebody for being who they are is the worst thing you can do. Even if you might not personally understand what it's like to be LGBTQ+, that's okay. You are building a closer bond with your child or loved one by being open and willing to learn about it for your child or loved one. You are demonstrating to them your love, compassion, and willingness to learn.

So how do I support my LGBTQ+ child, you ask? The solutions and strategies that follow will seem obvious, to be perfectly honest. Your child is, first and foremost, just a child, which is something you must always keep in mind. Your LGBTQ+ child is not an alien, whether they are little children or teenagers. They remain a regular child and a human being. They might have a different sexual orientation from you or a gender identification that differs from the one that corresponds to their assigned gender.

Make sure you are talking to your youngster. For instance, asking how their day at school was could suffice in this situation. Take an active role in your child's life.

That's not to mean you should smother them; rather, be actively involved in their lives. If a brawl broke out between their friends, ask them their thoughts on that. Discuss the altercation with them. Perhaps, they had been working extremely hard to get a particular part in the school play, but they ended up getting the understudy part. Ask them once more how they feel about that. Identify things that you can do to assist them. Possibly even assist them in memorizing their lines! Just take responsibility as a parent or family member.

You will build a relationship with your child if they feel at ease enough with you to discuss everyday issues like friend disputes and school plays. When they require you the most, such as when discussing sexuality, that relationship will deepen (Sanders & Fields, 2019). In all honesty, your child might approach you with inquiries regarding sex, such as how to engage in it properly, but they might also need to chat to you about that pretty lady in science class they have a crush on. If they don't want the name Julia that you gave them at birth, they can come to you and ask what you think about the name Dustin.

You'll discover that your child will feel at ease enough to talk to you about the most important things if you remain open to conversation and consistently demonstrate your love and acceptance for them. What a privilege! It's well known that talking to kids, especially teenagers, is challenging. But if you open up a line of contact early on, you'll discover that your child is more receptive and eager to have you involved in their lives.

But occasionally, despite our best efforts, our children may refuse to engage in conversation. Asking them simple questions is the most effective technique to start them talking. A great starting point would be to discuss possibly exciting things to them; perhaps they have a favorite music genre, artist, or group. Ask them about a song's lyrics; you might even want to know what they think the song is about. Further, if you have an LGBTQ+ child, take a causal stance while discussing sexuality. Perhaps, inquire if there are any LGBTQ+ members of the band. Ask them their thoughts on that. Maybe a character who identifies as LGBTQ+ appears in a show you are watching with your kid. How do people feel about that character? Do they believe the actor did a good job? (Sanders & Fields, 2019)

Additionally, keep in mind that there are some things you can say that could harm your child. Never suggest or imply that there is a "treatment" for being LGBTQ+ (Sanders & Fields, 2019). There is no ailment to treat. Being LGBTQ+ is just who we are; there is nothing wrong with it. In the same way, don't think of someone's sexuality as a phase (Sanders & Fields, 2019). Even though many people experiment with their sexuality, most people are attracted to certain types of people from an early age. The same is true for those of us who identify as transgender; many trans people have been aware of their gender identity since early childhood, even if they lack the words to describe their feelings at the time.

Suppose you dismiss someone's curiosity by calling it a phase. In that case, you are preparing your youngster to avoid talking to you or sharing things with you. Nevertheless, they attempt to express an essential feeling with you at that moment, so you must take these conversations carefully. That period of inquiry is crucial to them, even if they experiment and discover that they are heterosexual. During these trying moments, be there for your child or loved one. In all honestly, this is the best thing you can do for them.

Likewise, keep in mind that when your child comes out to you as LGBTQ+, nobody is to blame. They're not broken, and they don't need to be mended; if you indicate that someone is to blame, you're not trusting your child to know who they are. In addition to harming them because of their sexual orientation or gender identity, you will also cause them to lose confidence in themselves later in their lives. Instead of accepting responsibility for their successes and errors, they will place the blame on people around them.

To avoid placing blame, keep in mind that persons who identify as LGBTQ+ do not have to be that way voluntarily or under coercion. Instead, it is how they are from birth. Our only option is to be open and truthful about who we are and how we feel about ourselves. Denying our individuality is equivalent to denying our inner identity. You should keep in mind that there are numerous things you can do to assist your LGBTQ+ youngster as they adjust to school and life in general.

It is critical that you stand up for your child if you are their parent or legal guardian. Verify whether the GSA (Gay/Straight Alliance) group exists at your child's school. This will increase your child's school safety and help them meet new people (Sanders & Fields, 2019). Another action you may take is to demand better, more inclusive sex education from your child's school (Sanders & Fields, 2019).

The LGBTQ+ community is now widely discussed in schools, albeit these discussions are typically not as in-depth as those regarding linear relationships and sexual behavior. No matter who they may be having sex with, teaching our children about safe sex is crucial to keep them safe. Although it is vital to discuss transgender health, many schools ignore the problems that trans children face.

Regarding transgender health, your trans child must be allowed to use the proper bathroom. Gender-specific restrooms have been eliminated in certain schools, which is a positive step. Make sure there is a secure restroom for your child if the school has not done so. This could take the form of advocating for bathrooms open to people of all genders or for your trans son to be allowed to use the men's room.

Truthfully, your youngster will need to urinate and require that safe space. This was an essential topic in the press and media for a while. Additionally, your LGBTQ+ child will be more likely to experience bullying than cisgender or heterosexual youngsters (Sanders & Fields, 2019). Talk to your child if you find that they have grown distant or even overly sensitive. At your child's school or even during extracurricular activities, there can be something precarious going on behind your back.

Being observant on your part as a parent or guardian is vital. Keep an eye out for signs that your child is being bullied, such as a decline in grades, absenteeism, new friends, drug use, a rapid increase in sexual partners, and risk-taking behaviors like stealing or fighting (Sanders & Fields, 2019). When your child misbehaves, something is wrong in their life. If your child's behavior changes, keep an eye out for them.

Self-Love Is the Fruit of Self-Acceptance

I must say that we all could use a small reminder of how awesome and wonderful we are! I mean that with all my heart. Dr. Seuss, in all his wisdom, might also remind us that "Today you are you! That is truer than true! There is no one alive who is you-er than you! Shout loud, 'I am lucky to be what I am!'" We are indeed lucky to be who we are, and we must care for ourselves as much as we care for others.

A feeling of admiration for oneself that emerges from actions that advance our mental, emotional, and spiritual growth is known as self-love. To love yourself is to have great regard for your pleasure and well-being. Self-love implies taking care of your needs and avoiding endangering your health to appease others. A hallmark of self-love is refusing to accept anything less than you deserve. Self-love can mean different things to different individuals because we all have different methods of caring for ourselves. Understanding what self-love means to you depends on your mental health (Borenstein, 2020).

Self-love may be a personal practice for each person. For one person, self-love may entail speaking to and lovingly considering oneself and prioritizing oneself When you stop judging yourself, believe in yourself, or are honest with yourself, you show yourself love. It could also entail setting and upholding limits, admitting mistakes, or just being gracious to yourself in general. It might also imply respecting yourself (Borenstein, 2020).

Some people mistakenly use the word "self-care" in place of the phrase "self-love." These phrases are the same conceptually with different titles. Practicing self-love or self-care entails returning to the principles of self-care Self-love entails accepting and celebrating who you are right now, in this exact moment. It means prioritizing your physical, mental, and emotional well-being and embracing your emotions as they are (Borenstein, 2020).

It is important to be kind to yourself, above everything else. We are all human. We all make mistakes; therefore, every day is different. Not every action we take is going to be nice or kind to someone else. The best we can do is, very simply, to make every good faith effort. I am optimistic that this is going to take you closer to achieving the most acceptable version of who you want to be. Whatever you decide, you must embrace kindness and let it naturally flow from yourself and into the world around you to fulfill your obligation to love yourself.

Your life is the only one that exists. That is the plain truth of the situation. You, and no one else, must take steps to improve your life if you are unhappy with how it is. You must be the one to change your course if you feel that you are not moving in the right direction. Nobody else can carry it out for you. Yes, some people will support you, but ultimately you must put forth the effort to speak up for yourself and your demands.

Try to avoid feeling guilty about how your decision to live authentically has impacted others. You cannot punish yourself for doing the right thing. You may feel awful about witnessing the emotional struggles that your parents, siblings, and other people close to you are having. Even though widespread, such thoughts as "I wish things didn't have to be this way" or "I wish I didn't exist" are useless, destructive, and untrue. When you allow yourself to be aware of your feelings without categorizing them as happy or bad, tension is reduced, and you feel more in control. It's simpler to make decisions when you're not as anxious. You need to accept yourself as the same person you were before, but with more assurance in who you are right now.

Your experience improves when you take the time to reflect on the positive aspects of the day. So, every day or week, try to recall one good thing. Despite its small size, this lovely thing, whether it is "today was a bright day" or "my favorite blouse was clean," is real. It is significant, and it has the potential to change your perspective on life in general.

Consider this: you possess a jar. One giant boulder can fill that jar, which would be a significant feat. That is fantastic, but there is no longer any room left in the pot. Additionally, the smaller stones will take up more space in that jar collectively, making the jar heavier in the end. While it's vital, if not necessary, to celebrate life's milestones, the lesser achievements are just as significant. However, suppose you mark the minor victories as well. In that case, you will have overall had more celebrations than if you had only celebrated the more notable achievements.

This is related to showing yourself kindness and engaging in self-love or self-care. Discover one good thing about yourself every day if you can't find one good thing about the day. This might be as straightforward as the way your hair looked today. It could also be something more significant like you did an excellent job today on a task at work or school. Perhaps, you understood something that no one else could or marked the first time you were able to run a full mile without stopping and accomplished another milestone. You may have just finished knitting a blanket you've worked on for years. In any event, give yourself a pat on the back for your achievements. You are aware of what you did today and how it affected you. Practice focusing on the positive aspects of life, particularly the good qualities you possess.

Going back to Dr. Seuss' quote, I can say that I am fortunate to be who I am. Still, while destiny played a role, my decision to put myself first this time had a significant effect in my receiving that wonderful message. Our capacity to bestow on ourselves the compassion and goodness we have all desired must be expressed now. There is no better day than today.

LGBTQ+ people have a lot in common throughout their lives, including going against the grain, beating the odds, enduring heartbreak, overcoming fear, experiencing internal conflicts to varying degrees and for varying lengths of time, constantly making existential decisions, and much more. We also try to maintain a certain level of normalcy to contribute to society as active participants. That is a lot! After listing these obstacles, the adage I previously used—that life is a marathon—could not be more accurate. After several years of running the marathon, I'm fairly positive you now possess the strength and endurance to continue. However, I believe that the situation has changed. Because you have joined a group of survivors who refuse to be considered victims, you are taking back what has been properly yours all along. Your genuine, actual self. Your true, authentic self.

There are lots of things to appreciate about you. I'm happy for you because you can now take the time to finally put the puzzle pieces together from your visioning process. You are taking action, little by little, to plant seeds and witness your forward progress. You won't have to constantly reflect on happier times in the past. Instead, you may look forward to experiencing many more joyful moments in the future. Whether these times are spent by yourself, with someone else, with a group of friends, or while giving back to your community, witnessing your own happiness, and letting it spill over for others to feel is loving yourself.

So, being the first to stand up for yourself when you need to be is a sign of self-love. Self-love entails first filling one's own cup with the surplus intended for sharing with others. As they say, you can't pour anything from an empty cup. Wow, what a beautiful thing to go through.

What an incredible conclusion to accept. What a wonderful approach to honoring self-acceptance.

It's Okay to Talk to Someone

You can either fix your automobile yourself when it breaks down or find someone who can. While emotions can be changed, this is not always the case. You cannot pick up a wrench or take your sentiments to a repair shop. However, talking about your feelings is one technique you can always employ in your arsenal. It can be helpful to simply express your feelings to someone else. So why do we steer clear of it or think it is ineffective? Many factors can make it challenging to discuss our difficulties. Some individuals are conditioned to internalize their emotions rather than express them. The feelings you're experiencing, such as guilt over something you did or embarrassment over how you believe others view you, might occasionally feel so overwhelming that you lack the willpower to talk about them.

Talking offers tremendous psychological advantages that might not be clear, regardless of why you might choose to keep it inside. But let's go more specific because "talking about it" is a general term. It might take a few different shapes when we talk about talking about your difficulties (Ravenscraft, 2020). I am aware that the word "therapy" may provoke unpleasant memories for some people. You, however, are free to decide how you feel about it. It's appropriate to talk to someone, whether a trusted friend, family member or professional.

It is very appropriate to share your newly discovered happiness, hope, and excitement with someone. I believe it's a technique to see if you see and feel how you say you do. I'll repeat the adage, "You may fool others, but you cannot fool yourself." I mention this again to stress that you are a work in progress. I didn't transform overnight, and neither will you. I still have anxieties and doubts. We are not the only ones who can experience this; anyone who has achieved or is working toward achieving self-acceptance can.

Realizing self-acceptance for me means allowing myself to be excited and at peace with the knowledge that not everyone supported me on my new journey and that certain emotional triggers will continue to be a part of my everyday life. To help and legitimize the needs of people who identify as members of sexual and gender minorities, a type of psychotherapy known as affirmative therapy was developed. Using both verbal and nonverbal cues, therapists work with lesbian, gay, bisexual, and transgender (LGBT) clients to adopt a supportive stance (Hinrichs & Donaldson, 2017).

Support Resources

There's no moving appreciation for the present without acknowledging the lessons of the past. Lesbian, bisexual, and gay people had historically been subjected to discriminatory psychotherapy practices until the recent emergence of gay-affirmative therapy. It offers a practice paradigm that affirms lesbian, gay, and bisexual identities. Today, lesbian, gay, bisexual, transgender, queer, plus (LGBTQ+) persons may benefit from affirmative therapy.

The approach promotes a positive view of LGBTQ+ identities and relationships. It addresses the detrimental effects that homophobia, transphobia, and heterosexism (the presumption that all people are straight) have on LGBTQ+ people's lives (Carlson & McGeorge, 2010). We are now aware of what a heteronormative society is and its effects on individuals. We can hopefully see the disconnect in society's acknowledgment of the existence of individual and uniquely human qualities and characteristics, including human sexuality.

Furthermore, since heterosexual partnerships are the cultural norm, anything uncommon is strange. Yes, both globally and in the West, things are changing swiftly. The way that society views cultural diversity is evolving. The Defense of Marriage Act (DOMA) and the military's "don't ask, don't tell" policy have both been overturned, and religious orthodoxy may be changing. There is a growing intolerance of terms like "faggot," "homo," and "dyke." Gay marriage is now legal, and more common— but this doesn't mean that those whose sexual orientation and/or gender identification deviates from the norm suddenly have it easy.

On the contrary, LGBTQ+ people deal with bewilderment regarding who, what, why, and how they are different from others and from within. Even psychotherapists can lack a basic knowledge of what it means to be LGBTQ+ and those who do frequently bring a lifetime of cultural prejudice to the therapy session (Weiss, 2014).

Although statistics about LGBTQ+ mental health, violence, trauma, and harm have been discussed throughout this book, they're worth repeating from time to time because the numbers are concerning. LGBTQ+ adolescents are often well-adjusted and mentally healthy, as the Institute of Medicine has found. However, compared to their heterosexual friends, they have higher rates of mental health issues and more health consequences due to those issues.

Less research has been done on the outcomes for transgender youth compared to lesbian, gay, and bisexual youth. Up to one-third of self-identified transgender people in previous non-random surveys have admitted to trying to terminate their lives at least once, with rates among youth and young adults being more significant than those among older adults. In addition, LGBTQ+ kids are more prone than their classmates to try suicide, and suicide is the third most common cause of death among young people aged 15 to 24 (Youth.gov, 2022)

However, this does not imply that LGBTQ+ identification in and of itself is the root of these difficulties. Instead, these higher rates may be brought on by prejudice, discrimination, rejection from family members, and other stressors connected to how they are treated. Simply because of their sexual orientation or gender identity, or expression. These difficulties— referred to by researchers as "microaggressions"—can exacerbate anxiety, sadness, other mental-health issues, suicide, and other self-destructive behavior. Lesbian, homosexual, and bisexual kids are far more likely than their heterosexual counterparts to harbor suicidal thoughts, according to research.

According to recent studies, the reported rates of suicide attempts among high school students who identify as LGBTQ+ are also two to seven times higher than the reported rates among heterosexual high school students. Youth who identify as LGBTQ+ are also twice as likely to consider suicide (Youth.gov, 2022). The task to combat these staggering numbers belong to all of us in the LGBTQ+ community across the globe and in partnerships with our community resources and groups.

A fantastic resource for LGBTQ+ people, especially young people who are experiencing mental-health crises or are suicidal, is The Trevor Project. Volunteers take the time to listen to callers and help them get into a more secure frame of mind. Additionally, they provide lobbying, research, public education, and peer support. On top of that, their website offers a safe way for you to quickly leave if you're not in a place where the community welcomes LGBTQ+ concerns or if you haven't come out to your family.

•The Trevor Project's website: https://www.thetrevorproject.org/

Resources for LGBTQ+ people are far more plentiful now than in the past. This is a terrific step forward when you require help but cannot get it from friends or family. Parents, Families, and Friends of Lesbians and Gays (PFLAG) is an excellent additional resource for LGBTQ+ people. The largest group devoted to assisting, educating, and promoting the rights of LGBTQ+ persons and their families is PFLAG, created in 1973. PFLAG was the first organization of its kind and continues to be so today (PFLAG, 2019). They offer support for LGBTQ+ people, their families, and friends via their website, providing detailed information on what it means to be LGBTQ+. On the website, there are pages with details on laws that apply to the LGBTQ+ community and instructions on how to launch or join a local PFLAG chapter.

•The PFLAG website: https://pflag.org/

•The PFLAG Support Hotlineshttps://pflag.org/hotlines

On its website, 988 Suicide and Crisis Lifeline, formerly known as the National Suicide Prevention Lifeline, provides a section dedicated to supporting LGBTQ+ people who are experiencing a crisis. This contains details and advice for allies on how to support their LGBTQ+ family members. A comprehensive list of additional resources is also included, including GLAAD and Planned Parenthood.

•The 988 Suicide and Crisis Lifeline LGBTQ+ page: https://988lifeline.org/help-yourself/lgbtq/

A page on mental health services for LGBTQ+ people and their friends and relatives can be found on the Human Rights Council website. This website provides links and phone information for several hotlines that can assist LGBTQ+ people experiencing a difficult time.

•The Human Rights Council's Mental Health Resources for LGBTQ+: https://www.hrc.org/resources/mental-health-resources-in-the-lgbtq-community

Sometimes, asking for assistance can be the most difficult thing we have to do. Given that we are socially conditioned to be independent, admitting that we need help can be stressful in and of itself. Despite this attitude, asking for assistance is not a sign of weakness. It is, if anything, a strength. You are demonstrating to the world that you are prepared to work through your problems rather than just giving up by expressing, "I need help."

You are a unique person who deserves respect and compassion. Receiving that can be challenging at times, particularly if you are in a dangerous circumstance. No matter what time of day it is, you can get assistance from the hotlines and websites mentioned above. If you feel the slightest need for assistance, please get in touch with one of them. You should also tell your loved ones about the websites so they can learn more about what it's like to be LGBTQ+ and how they may support you.

After reading this book, I sincerely hope that you will be willing to let support networks and groups help you when you most need it. Your journey toward self-acceptance offers you a fantastic opportunity to use some of your darkest experiences as a reminder of prior struggles you overcame to become the self-sufficient, resilient person you are now. Your hands deserve to be held in support and love. Do you recall the discussion on the impact of our shared stories? You can share them here so that other people can listen, be inspired, and learn.

It's Nice to Meet You

You have my appreciation for getting here. You started with the first step, thanks to your guts and your self-confidence. Thanks to your strength, you have successfully completed the first part of your journey despite the physical, mental, and emotional challenges. You have made room in your head for a wide range of possibilities, some of which were out of your wildest dreams. Simply to receive and live your full, authentic self this time, you dared to be different.

Let me say again that this is not the end of your journey. Like those who have climbed Mount Everest, reaching each campsite merits its own victory. For some, reaching the summit is the goal, but only a few have managed to achieve that goal. For others, they carried their promises to themselves or others, and the mere trek alone was the fulfillment of that promise. Although your journey to self-acceptance has similarities to climbing Mount Everest, your summit is simply to live daily.

Your goal of daily living is your summit, even though your path to self-acceptance resembles Mount Everest. There may be days when you don't feel like you're moving forward on a mountain, yet you may be. Sometimes you believe that you have completed all of the tasks at hand; on those days, you will feel the most self-assured and loved. But, then, there may be times when you feel as though you have hit your lowest point; these are the times when you may be least able to love yourself. Never forget that you are not the same person you were when you began this adventure hundreds of miles ago.

Occasionally, I see these instances as indicative of my re-emergence as a proud homosexual guy who is fortunate enough to be alive in this day and age and happily share his story, just like everyone else. Yet, you have the strength, the clarity of vision, the joy for life, the appreciation of love, the drive to motivate others, and the daily discipline of living an authentic life. Best of all, you are a person who has achieved self-acceptance with a dedication to living your best life.

Bear in mind that your journey is something you must continue throughout the rest of your life; it is never truly finished. While it may seem like a huge undertaking, you are not walking that far. Yes, a voyage is involved, but you can take your time. Walking great distances is not always necessary; sometimes, just one step will do. You can feel like you are moving backward or standing still sometimes. Remember your progress throughout those times. Consider your starting position and the distance you have traveled since then. For example, one foot, one mile, or one step. The joy you experience on your voyage matters, not how many steps you take.

Along the way, you will meet people who want to help you. Unfortunately, you will also meet people who dislike or even despise you simply because you are being true to yourself. These people may cause you to reconsider your course of action. On the other hand, you might be paying too close attention to them.

Whatever the case may be, do not let them alter your course. You've carved out your own path. Being yourself is precisely what you need to do right now. Realizing that the best thing you can do is to be true to yourself will bring you more joy than anything else. With this new boldness, pride, courage, and a strong sense of self, be mindful to not miss out on an opportunity to assist others. Leaving the past behind does not mean forgetting where you came from.

Instead, feed your soul with acts that uplift others that are even more meaningful when it's only you and the person who has knowledge of the kindness you've shown. People are sometimes intricately placed in our lives. They come to us because one or both of you are unaware of them at the time. These special people have an impact on you. They alter your soul, change your perspective, and leave an imprint on your heart. You now have a special relationship with compassion because, at some point, kindness was extended to you just when you needed it most.

For me, the most moving part of any journey is the conclusion. The entire time I was writing this book, I traveled beside you on your long trip, whether you were listening to it or reading it. You were an imaginary buddy when I was navigating the waters of sharing stories to self-acceptance. You gave me a reflected mirror of my existence. But I also earnestly hope our voyage together has served as your self-reflective mirror, devoid of opinions and any unreliable depictions of events or people, just transparency and clarity.

The hills and valleys of any life journey are something I've talked about a lot in this book. There will undoubtedly be challenging and perhaps lonely periods. But I hope the stories you heard, the lessons you learned, the words that spoke to you, and the satisfaction of accepting who you are will fill your cup when you're in need. Maintain your new connections while they get to know the new you. They belong to your family. You won't ever be left alone again. The unattributed quote "Family is not always blood" sums it up perfectly. It's the individuals that accept you for who you are and want you in their lives. Those who are devoted to you would do anything to make you happy. Those who are unwavering in their devotion to you and sacrifice anything to see you smile. You are responsible for the remainder, so do as your heart desires.

My chosen family is here. I feel blessed to have a husband who is prepared to walk by my side through the toughest times and loves me without conditions. We have been faithful to one another for more than ten years, and I fervently pray that our love will continue to sustain us till the end of our days. I also have wonderful friends I firmly believe came into my life precisely at the right time. I've known most of them for almost 20 years, and since the first time I met them, I've felt a true acceptance. They are my brothers and sisters. When the sun rises the following day, they will still be there despite having witnessed many of my worst times. I yearn for the day when we can speak again, even though we don't talk every day.

I'm only one of many people that are rooting for you. I'm happy to claim that, even briefly, I knew you while you continued your journey. You have permitted me to travel with you on a metaphorical journey by choosing to read this book, and I am grateful for that. You exposed yourself to vulnerability by returning to old sentiments, memories, experiences, and emotions, even if you weren't sure how it may affect you. But given that you're reading the final sentences of this book, I hope they were as liberating for you as they were for me.

Unhiding my skin to self-acceptance was, without a doubt, the most unbinding experience of my life. It gave me the privilege and the wonderful gift of living authentically, loving proudly, and inspiring greatly.

Although we have never met in person, I had a vision of the reader of this book since I am just like you.

I am grateful and honored to meet you.

Welcome!

Conclusion

This book was written as a love letter to the LGBTQ+ community, which you are a part of. As LGBTQ+, I hope that you've added insight into your identity. As an ally, my prayer is that you have begun understanding the struggles of your LGBTQ+ friends or family. Together, my wish is that you appreciate the freedom of what it means to live each day as yourself. Your journey of discovery will be ongoing until we leave this earth. Enjoy savoring the gift of breathing, living, and freedom each day. Mindfully be in awe of continuing to evolve beautifully as a person unburdened by the shadows of hiding your skin. This book is a tool that was purposefully crafted for your journey to self-acceptance.

Please lend this book to a friend or family member who is going through similar difficulties now that you have finished reading it. Then, continue to spread the love. As a butterfly emerges from its cocoon, assist someone else in revealing their skin and spreading their wings. Take a moment to look around you and reflect on where you started and where you are right now. You began by learning to love and accept yourself before delicately moving on to discovering the finest possible way to live your life. You have found that there are people who love you and are ready to support you. During challenging times, you know you have a community network of resources. Now it's your turn to assist someone else while continuing to in your own development.

The lessons and stories in this book have taken you this far. Now it's your turn to go out into the world and improve your life and the lives of those around you by simply choosing not to hide who you are. Keep in mind to pursue your happiness. Never forget to rejoice every day and celebrate your daily wins.

Your opportunity to shine has arrived, and you have the green light to take action. You dared to be different, and you crossed paths with people who share your story toward self-acceptance. You also met those who have already made the necessary strides and are ready to support you. You came to understand that you dared not just to be different but also great. You have taken responsibility for your actions and have had the guts to live your truth. Therefore, keep striving to be the best version of yourself while learning and developing every day. Be a light in the lives of those around you and your own every day.

Your worth and affection are recognized. Nothing in our lives happens that doesn't lead us to where we should be. Everything will work out for you because you have prepared yourself. Be sure to keep your shoulders back and your chin up. You are now the hope whose shoulders others after you will stand on.

Unhiding your skin is the legacy you leave behind for a life purposefully lived, sustained by love that will be remembered by everyone you inspired.

About the Author

Dr. Carl Carado holds a Doctor of Education, Juris Doctor, and a master's degree in Nursing, in addition to being licensed as a registered nurse for over 25 years. He is a proud military veteran and considers it an honor and a privilege to have served in the U.S. Army and U.S. Air Force. Carl struggled as a teen with his sexuality and continues to deal with societal and family acceptance issues as an adult. He has dedicated many years to attempt to figure out his place in society while navigating internal conflicts related to faith, race, relationships, and self-acceptance. As a result, he endured emotional, physical, and psychological abuse, depression, and shame. His passion for helping others get to a place of self-acceptance is now one of his lifelong missions. Today, he stands in sharing the message that our most incredible armor is self-acceptance and living our authentic lives fearlessly.

In Carl's opinion, one of the bravest things you can accomplish as an individual is to accept who you are, regardless of what others may think. He joins the countless others who have shared their experiences of the suffering brought on by being a gay person of color or by living outside of the heterosexual conventions of society. With the help of this book, he hopes to show you that you are not alone and that by standing up each day, you stop the cycle of hiding. As a result, you will overcome your obstacles and will go on to encourage others to do the same.

References

American Psychiatric Association. (n.d.). *LGBTQ*. Www.psychiatry.org.https://www.psychiatry.org/psychiatrists/cultural-competency/education/stress-and-trauma/lgbtq

Anon. (n.d.). *Someone Who Will Love You in All Your Damaged Glory Quotes by Raphael Bob-Waksberg*. Www.goodreads.com. Retrieved November 3, 2022, from https://www.goodreads.com/work/quotes/65449883-someone-who-will-love-you-in-all-your-damaged-glory-stories

Asakura, K. (2016). Paving Pathways Through the Pain: A Grounded Theory of Resilience Among Lesbian, Gay, Bisexual, Trans, and Queer Youth. *Journal of Research on Adolescence, 27*(3), 521–536. https://doi.org/10.1111/jora.12291

ASAP. (n.d.). *The American Society of Administrative Professionals*. Www.asaporg.com. Retrieved November 3, 2022, from https://www.asaporg.com

beaconmm. (2022, April 21). *How To Love Yourself: Pursuing Self-Acceptance & Forgiveness*. Ellie Mental Health, PLLP. https://elliementalhealth.com/how-to-love-yourself-a-journey-toward-self-acceptance-and-forgiveness/

Beck, M. (2014, August). *7 Ways to Spark a Major Breakthrough in Your Life*. Oprah.com.

https://www.oprah.com/omagazine/how-to-have-a-breakthrough-in-your-life/all

Bennett-Rylah, J. (2021, June 1). *17 Contemporary LGBTQIA+ Writers to Read Now.* Notable Contemporary LGBTQIA+ Writers | Grammarly Blog. https://www.grammarly.com/blog/contemporary-lgbtqia-writers/

Berman, R. (2021, July 20). *For LGBTQ+ people of faith: Fear of rejection meets joy of inclusion.* Www.medicalnewstoday.com. https://www.medicalnewstoday.com/articles/lgbtq-people-of-faith-rejection-and-healing#The-joy-of-inclusion

Borenstein, J. (2020, February 12). *Self-Love and What It Means.* Brain & Behavior Research Foundation. https://www.bbrfoundation.org/blog/self-love-and-what-it-means

Brach, T. (2017, March). *Radical Self-Honesty | Psychology Today.* Www.psychologytoday.com. https://www.psychologytoday.com/us/blog/finding-true-refuge/201703/radical-self-honesty

Bregman, H. R., Malik, N. M., Page, M. J. L., Makynen, E., & Lindahl, K. M. (2012). Identity Profiles in Lesbian, Gay, and Bisexual Youth: The Role of Family Influences. *Journal of Youth and Adolescence, 42*(3), 417–430. https://doi.org/10.1007/s10964-012-9798-z

Catherine, L. (2019, August 28). *Why you need people: The benefits of community.* Choose to See Good.

https://choosetoseegood.com/why-you-need-people-the-benefits-of-community/

CCARE Staff. (2012, December 14). *Self-Compassion - The Center for Compassion and Altruism Research and Education.* The Center for Compassion and Altruism Research and Education. http://ccare.stanford.edu/research/wiki/comp assion-definitions/self-compassion/

Common Sense Media. (2020, June). *What is courage? | Common Sense Media.* www.commonsensemedia.org. https://www.commonsensemedia.org/articles/ what-is-courage

Cy, S. (2019, March 14). *Why Other People's Opinions Matter…And What to Do When They Make You Feel Bad.* Publishous. https://medium.com/publishous/why-other-peoples-opinions-matter-and-what-to-do-when-they-make-you-feel-bad-ab337ebdc98e

Daskal, L. (2016, May 12). *How to Stop Worrying What Other People Think of You.* Inc.com. https://www.inc.com/lolly-daskal/how-to-stop-worrying-what-other-people-think-of-you.html

Doctor D. (n.d.). *10 Easy Ways to Nurture Yourself with Self Care.* Sparkling Probiotic Drink | Doctor D's. https://www.doctordslive.com/health-

wellbeing/10-easy-ways-to-nurture-yourself-
with-self-care

Drescher, J. (2015). Out of DSM: Depathologizing
homosexuality. *Behavioral Sciences*, *5*(4), 565–575.
https://doi.org/10.3390/bs5040565

Dunmore. (2017, April 25). *The Importance of Having
Strong Communities*. Dunmore Borough
Pennsylvania.
https://dunmorepa.gov/news/importance-
strong-
communities/#:~:text=Having%20a%20sense
%20of%20community

Earnshaw, E. (2019, February). *The Power of Your
Personal Narrative*. A Better Life Therapy.
https://abetterlifetherapy.com/blog/the-
power-of-your-personal-narrative

Foroux, D. (2016, October 3). *The Purpose Of Life Is Not
Happiness: It's Usefulness*. Darius Foroux.
https://dariusforoux.com/happiness-
usefulness/

Fredrickson, B. L. (2001). *APA PsycNet*.
Psycnet.apa.org.
https://psycnet.apa.org/doiLanding?doi=10.10
37%2F0003-
066X.56.3.218&utm_source=elliotlaketoday.co
m&utm_campaign=elliotlaketoday.com&tm_m
edium=referral

Hagaman, J. S. and J. (2019). *Identifying emotional triggers
leads to better self awareness*. Sarasota Herald-
Tribune.
https://www.heraldtribune.com/story/news/lo
cal/manatee/2019/07/08/identifying-

emotional-triggers-leads-to-better-self-
awareness/4745208007/

Harvard Health Publishing. (2019). *The power of self-
compassion - Harvard Health*. Harvard Health;
Harvard Health.
https://www.health.harvard.edu/healthbeat/th
e-power-of-self-compassion

Hinrichs, K. L. M., & Donaldson, W. (2017). *Living
Authentically as Lesbian, Gay and Bisexual+*. HRC.
https://www.hrc.org/resources/coming-out-
living-authentically-as-lesbian-gay-and-bisexual

How To Be At Peace With Yourself. (2019, June 15). The
Joy Within. https://thejoywithin.org/increase-
happiness/how-to-be-at-peace-with-yourself

Human Rights Campaign. (2011, August 17). *Faith
Positions | Human Rights Campaign*. Human
Rights Campaign.
https://www.hrc.org/resources/faith-positions

Kanaloupiti, F. (2018). *"Mirror, mirror on the wall…": Why
other people's opinion matters so much?* ANTI-
LONELINESS.
https://www.antiloneliness.com/self-
development/mirror-mirror-on-the-wall-why-
other-peoples-opinion-matters-so-much

KY COUNSELING CENTER. (2021, April 16). *How
to Find Your "Inner Peace."* Kentucky Counseling
Center.
https://kentuckycounselingcenter.com/how-to-
find-inner-peace/

Lataille, N., & O'Neill, H. (n.d.). *The evolution of LGBTQ
inclusion: Building cultures of greater acceptance and*

stronger communities. www.heidrick.com. https://www.heidrick.com/en/insights/diversity-inclusion/the-evolution-of-lgbtq-inclusion

Lee, A. M. I. (2014). *Self-Advocacy: What It Is and Why It's Important*. www.understood.org. https://www.understood.org/en/articles/the-importance-of-self-advocacy

LGBTQ+. (n.d.). 988lifeline.org. https://988lifeline.org/help-yourself/lgbtq/Marschall, A. (2022). *Why You Might Feel Unlovable and How to Cope*. Verywell Mind. https://www.verywellmind.com/why-you-might-feel-unlovable-and-how-to-cope-5215404

Merriam-Webster Dictionary. (n.d.). *Definition of RADICAL*. Www.merriam-Webster.com. Retrieved November 3, 2022, from https://www.merriam-webster.com/dictionary/radical?utm_campaign=sd&utm_medium=serp&utm_source=jsonld

Miller, K. (2019, July 4). *What is Kindness in Psychology? (Incl. Activities + Quotes)*. PositivePsychology.com. https://positivepsychology.com/character-strength-kindness/

Morandini, J. S., Costa, A., Godwin, D. S. J., & Dar-Nimrod, I. (2017). *Born this way: Sexual orientation beliefs and their correlates in lesbian and bisexual women*. Psycnet.apa.org.

https://psycnet.apa.org/record/2017-16715-
001

Neff, K. (2003). Self-Compassion: An Alternative
Conceptualization of a Healthy Attitude
Toward Oneself. *Self and Identity*, *2*(2), 85–101.
https://doi.org/10.1080/15298860309032

Neff, K., & Germer, C. (2019, January 29). *The
Transformative Effects of Mindful Self-Compassion -
Mindful*. Mindful.
https://www.mindful.org/the-transformative-
effects-of-mindful-self-compassion/

NHS. (2018, November 20). *Mindfulness*. Nhs.uk.
https://www.nhs.uk/mental-health/self-
help/tips-and-support/mindfulness/

Olito, F. (2020). *11 inspiring stories of LGBTQ teenagers
that have moved the internet*. Insider.
https://www.insider.com/inspiring-stories-of-
lgbtq-high-school-teens-2020-6

Option B. (2009). *Why Accepting your LGBTQ Child
Matters—And How to Start*. OptionB.org.
https://optionb.org/articles/why-accepting-
your-lgbtq-child-matters-and-how-to-start

Page, M. J. L., Lindahl, K. M., & Malik, N. M. (2013).
The Role of Religion and Stress in Sexual
Identity and Mental Health Among Lesbian,
Gay, and Bisexual Youth. *Journal of Research on
Adolescence*, *23*(4), 665–677.
https://doi.org/10.1111/jora.12025

Pavlovitz, J. (2021, July). *Medium*. Medium.
https://medium.com/equality-includes-you/its-
courageous-to-%20be-lgbtq-and-in-the-closet-

too-74588adc99be PFLAG. (2019). *PFLAG.* Pflag.org. https://pflag.org/about

Planned Parenthood. (2022). *What causes sexual orientation?* www.plannedparenthood.org. https://www.plannedparenthood.org/learn/sexual-orientation/sexual-orientation/what-causes-sexual-orientation

Plata, M. (2018). *How to Spot Your Emotional Triggers.* Psychology Today. https://www.psychologytoday.com/us/blog/the-gen-y-psy/201810/how-spot-your-emotional-triggers

Psych Central. (2014, April 9). *Understanding LGBTQ-Affirmative Psychotherapy.* Psych Central. https://psychcentral.com/blog/sex/2014/04/understanding-lgbtq-affirmative-psychotherapy

Psychcentra. (2021, August 25). *Trauma and LGBTQIA+ Communities: What to Know.* Psych Central. https://psychcentral.com/lib/lgbt-suicide-and-the-trauma-of-growing-up-gay#protecting-youth

Ravenscraft, E. (2020, April 3). Why Talking About Our Problems Helps So Much (and How to Do It). *The New York Times.* https://www.nytimes.com/2020/04/03/smarter-living/talking-out-problems.html

Ryan, C. (2014). *A PrActitioner's resource Guide: Helping Families to Support Their LGBT Children AcKnoWLedGeMents.*

https://store.samhsa.gov/sites/default/files/d7/priv/pep14-lgbtkids.pdf

S, N. (2013). *Trevor: The Story that Inspired the Trevor Project*. Rainbow Round Table Book and Media Reviews. https://www.glbtrt.ala.org/reviews/trevor-the-story-that-inspired-the-trevor-project/

Sanders, R., & Fields, E. L. (2019). *Tips for Parents of LGBTQ Youth*. Johns Hopkins Medicine. https://www.hopkinsmedicine.org/health/wellness-and-prevention/tips-for-parents-of-lgbtq-youth

Sandstrom, A. (2015, December 2). *Religious groups' policies on transgender members vary widely*. Pew Research Center; Pew Research Center. https://www.pewresearch.org/fact-tank/2015/12/02/religious-groups-policies-on-transgender-members-vary-widely/

Saxe, R. (2017, December 1). *It's Always Been About Discrimination for LGBT People | News & Commentary*. American Civil Liberties Union. https://www.aclu.org/news/lgbtq-rights/its-always-been-about-discrimination-lgbt-people

Selby, D. (2018, June 22). *15 LGBTQ Activists of the Past and Present You Should Know*. Global Citizen. https://www.globalcitizen.org/en/content/lgbtq-pride-activists-advocates-johnson-milk/

Seltzer, L. F. (2011). *The Path to Unconditional Self-Acceptance*. Psychology Today. https://www.psychologytoday.com/us/blog/ev

olution-the-self/200809/the-path-
unconditional-self-acceptance

Seuss, D. (2020, June 24). *Just Being Who We Are:
Personal Stories from Our LGBTQ Community.*
What's Next.
https://whatsnext.nuance.com/life-at-
nuance/just-being-who-we-are-personal-stories-
from-our-lgbtq-community/

Stevens, T. G. (2021). *Part 3:Self-Acceptance.*
Home.csulb.edu.
https://home.csulb.edu/~tstevens/h53accep.ht
m

Stewart, C. (2019, December 9). *Radical Honesty: How To
Live With Authentic Truth.* Insight Timer Blog.
https://insighttimer.com/blog/how-to-start-
living-with-radical-honesty/

The Trevor Project. (n.d.-a). *Navigating LGBTQ Identities
and Religion.* The Trevor Project.
https://www.thetrevorproject.org/resources/ar
ticle/navigating-lgbtq-identities-and-religion/

The Trevor Project. (n.d.-b). *Volunteer with The Trevor
Project.* The Trevor Project. Retrieved
November 3, 2022, from
https://www.thetrevorproject.org/volunteer/?g
clid=CjwKCAjwp9qZBhBkEiwAsYFsb9rWrW
gna6knYXOQG23cdadu3wU-
DB9C4_z5d4dkN_qEqYBiQ-
YzBoCHrcQAvD_BwE

UCL. (2020, December 5). *7 ways you can be a better
LGBTQ+ ally.* Students.

https://www.ucl.ac.uk/students/news/2020/dec/7-ways-you-can-be-better-lgbtq-ally

UK Research and Innovation. (2018). *LGBTQ Visions of Peace in a Society Emerging.* Ukri.org. https://gtr.ukri.org/projects?ref=AH%2FN008588%2F1

Wagaman, M. A., Obejero, R. C., & Gregory, J. S. (2018). Countering the Norm, (Re)authoring Our Lives. *International Journal of Qualitative Methods, 17*(1), 160940691880064. https://doi.org/10.1177/1609406918800646

Washington, J. (2021, April 12). *Born again doesn't mean what others portray it to be.* The Atlanta Voice. https://theatlantavoice.com/born-again-doesnt-mean-what-others-portray-it-to-be/

Youth.gov. (2019). *Behavioral Health | Youth.gov.* Youth.gov; Youth.gov. https://youth.gov/youth-topics/lgbtq-youth/health-depression-and-suicide